Contents

CW00820053

The Olympic Games is undoubtedly the greatest show on earth. Held every four years, no other event draws so many sportsmen and women together from all over the world for three weeks of sport, attracting more than 200,000 live spectators each day, plus the billions watching on television.

For many athletes, the Olympics is the pinnacle of their sporting careers. To win a gold medal is the dream of many who spend several years in rigorous training, personal sacrifice and hard work. Yet there is only one gold medal to aspire to in each event, and so many will fall short of their lifelong ambitions. Nevertheless, as encapsulated in the Olympic creed (written by its modern founder, Baron Pierre de Coubertin):

'The most important thing in the Olympic Games is not to win but to take part, just as the most important thing in life is not the triumph but the struggle. The essential thing is not to have conquered but to have fought well.'

The essence of this creed stems from the view that, if athletes strive to perform well and have become accomplished to the best of their ability in their chosen sport, they are just as worthy of recognition as the one who actually wins the gold medal.

Although in reality this may not be the view of most Olympians today, whose only desire is to win the gold, the creed – as well as the entire Olympic ethos – carries a number of spiritual parallels.

The Christian 'race' is about participation, running well and claiming a reward at the end. We are called in Scripture to 'run with patience' (Hebrews 12:1), to 'press on toward the goal' (Philippians 3:14) and to 'endure to the end' (Mark 13:13). In the Christian 'race', there is no rank order of positions, and everyone who takes part in this special race can be a winner. There are no losers for those who are in Christ.

So, in a similar way to the Olympic creed, for a Christian the most important thing is to take part in the Christian race – for by doing so you become a winner. By enduring the struggle you triumph – and, like the apostle Paul, who said, 'I have fought a good fight, I have finished my course' (2 Timothy 4:7, KJV) – if we have fought well, we will conquer.

I have been fortunate in attending the last three Olympic Games – Sydney, Athens and Beijing – working as a chaplain and volunteer. As a Christian observing the whole Olympic scene, I am always amazed at the spiritual lessons and inspiring acts of bravery that take place during its sessions. Watching the highs of triumphant performances as well as the lows of athletes missing out on victory has also taught me many object lessons: hurdlers stumbling at the last hurdle, unknown Olympians outshining the firm favourites, and the crowd's warm response to those who struggle but eventually cross the finishing line, albeit in last place.

It is all these acts of Olympic heroism and disappointment that have inspired me to write this book and compare them to our service and walk with God. It is my aim to provide encouragement and direction as to how we can participate in the race God has called us to run, so that in the end we will receive a reward that is worth far more than gold.

chapter one

Start the race
Beginning the journey

Suddenly I turned around and looked up at the clock. I had one minute to get on the plane! I had always considered myself to be a pretty fast runner, so even in this situation I thought I might still have a chance. I was at Los Angeles Airport, one of the largest airports in the world. The plane was boarding at gate sixty-five, and I was only at gate five! Like a decathlete, I sprinted as fast as I could along the corridor, high-jumping over baggage and pole-vaulting over prams. Bounding along, I strained every sinew in my body to get there on time.

When I finally arrived at gate sixty-five nobody was there. My heart was beating so fast it seemed in a race of its own, fuelled by the adrenaline still pumping through my body. 'Was I too late?' I thought fearfully, yet in the hope that there was still a chance. I went over to the door that led down the passageway to the plane. It was slightly open and I pushed to go through it, only to be met by a flight attendant who stopped me with an adamant 'Sorry, but you can't get on the plane!'

'But I'm supposed to be on that plane', I replied desperately.

'Sorry', he said with a firm voice, holding up his hand so as to bar my way.

'The door of the plane is closed and the engines have already started.'

'But I've got my luggage on that plane!' I exclaimed desperately, 'Plus my hand luggage, with all my money, and I have a connecting flight to catch!'

'As I said,' he replied, as determined as ever, 'you're too late; the door of the plane is closed.'

I was totally gobsmacked! I looked out of the large glass window facing the runway and I could see my plane. To make things worse, I could even see the heads of those comfortably seated on the inside, while I was being left behind! I can't fully explain how I felt that day. It should never have happened. I had allowed myself to become distracted.

Just to backtrack – I was returning home to London after spending one year as a student missionary teaching in a mission school in the Marshall Islands of the Pacific Ocean. As a 19-year-old I had just experienced the time of my life. I had experienced God in a very personal way as a teacher in the mission school, and I had learnt to depend on, and trust in, God at a higher level than I had done before. When my year ended it was a sad thing to say goodbye to the children with whom I had developed such a close bond. They had taught me more about life than I could ever teach them. Sadly, it was time to return home.

My journey was quite a long one. The Marshall Islands are literally on the other side of the world from England, so the first section of my flight was from Majuro, the capital of the Marshall Islands, to Hawaii. The next day the journey continued from Hawaii to New York, with a flight time of over twelve hours. I had prepared myself for this. I needed some rest, and this was a good opportunity for it. Five hours into the journey, an announcement was made by the pilot that the plane would be stopping off in LA for refuelling, and that we would be able to leave the plane if needed to take a break and 'stretch our legs'. We were told that the stop would only be for an hour.

I thought this was a good opportunity to look around the airport. At least I could say that I'd been to LA. We were each given a transit card and told to come back to gate sixty-five to continue the rest of the flight.

Los Angeles airport is like a world of its own. The Marshall Islands, though among the most picturesque places in the world, could not be compared to the attractions and bright lights of what the airport had to offer. I came off the plane with my transit card in hand and began looking around the shops, catching up on the latest styles of fashion and browsing through the magazines. After a short while I went down the escalator and was awed by the mass of people from around the world, with different cultural clothes, and speaking various languages. I was totally engrossed in all this.

All of a sudden something said to me, 'Richard, look at the clock!' And that is how I ended up standing outside gate sixty-five, while my plane was taxiing off down the runway.

What I thought was just twenty minutes or so of looking around the airport had lapsed into an entire hour. I had been so caught up in the attractions of the airport, almost hypnotised, that momentarily I'd lost sight of the reality of time.

In the middle of my shock, fear and panic, the same flight attendant came over to me and explained that I could get the next plane, which would be departing in two hours.

This plane, however, would be going to LaGuardia Airport in Newark, about a two-hour drive from New York, instead of Kennedy Airport, which was my original destination. I had little choice; I was now on a different plane, going on a different journey, bound for a different destination.

Life is a journey

It sounds like a cliché, I know, but life is a journey. Every journey has a destination. As with any journey, it is obviously important to know where your destination is. Knowing where you are going makes all the difference in how you travel to get there.

Ultimately God's desire is that we choose the destination He has planned for us. His desire is that we all embark on a journey that is heavenward-bound. His words of invitation are clear: 'I go to prepare a place for you . . . I will come again . . . that where I am, there you may be also' (John 14:2, 3, NKJV).

Our final destination is to be with God and to live with Him in the place that He has prepared for each of us. As Christian experienced in the book *Pilgrim's Progress*, there will be obstacles and challenges designed to distract us and turn us away from the right path – but we are urged to remain faithful and focused. Psalm 32:8 (in the Living Bible) says:

'I will instruct you (says the Lord) and guide you along the best pathway for your life; I will advise you and watch your progress.'

The apostle Paul compared this journey to a race in which runners strive toward the goal of gaining the prize. During his many missionary travels, Paul became acquainted with athletic competitions (he would have been familiar with the Isthmian Games, held near Corinth), and no doubt often observed the way athletes prepared and trained for these events. He saw a natural parallel between the athlete's approach to his race and desire to win the crown, and that of the Christian and his desire to gain a crown of a more permanent kind. That's why he was able to pen these inspiring words:

'I have fought the good fight, I have finished the race, I have kept the faith. Finally, there is laid up for me the crown of righteousness . . .' (2 Timothy 4:7, 8, NKJV).

Choose life

The dynamics of this race are very much like my experience in trying to get to my destination. I wish I could say that it's all plain sailing along a rosy path. It's not. There may be times when we will be distracted and tempted to take our eyes off the goal, as in my case. There will be potential detours along that journey designed to take us along a completely different path to the one we intended. Attractions are placed along the way to hypnotise us; to cause us to lose our focus and numb our sensitivity to the reality of the time in which we live.

However, we all are called to choose life, to embark on a Christian race that not only leads to eternity but allows each one of us to experience a life of joy, peace and contentment. Jesus says, 'The thief comes only to steal and kill and destroy; I have come that they may have life, and have it to the full.' (John 10:10, NIV.)

Not only does God want you to live life to the full, but in this race He wants you to live a purpose-driven life. His personal words to you are:

' "For I know the plans I have for you," declares the LORD, "plans to prosper you and not to harm you, plans to give you hope and a future." ' (Jeremiah 29:11, NIV.)

No one knows you like God does. He's known about you since before time began. He was present at your birth and he's been intimately acquainted with every detail of your life right up till now. He's aware of your weaknesses as well as your strengths. He knows your fears and your joys. He knows how to make your life fulfilling and how to make it really count for something. That's why He has plans for you. He didn't create you just to abandon you to figure out life as you go along. He loves you far too much for that.

God has a perfect plan for your life. It's tailored just for you. It matches the things He's building into your character right now. The plan He has for you is not necessarily the same as His plans for your family or friends. The promises He has made to you and the things He has taught you are part of His design for your life.

How tragic to live your life and accomplish all your own goals, yet never discover what could have been if you had sought God's direction! He will show you options you never considered. You will have no regrets when you allow God to direct your steps, for His path leads to an abundant life.

Remember: your life is a part of God's grand design. God had a plan for your life since before time began. Your life, therefore, has a destiny. Christ is the Model upon which the Father is developing your life. You are meant to have a relationship with the Father that is as intimate as the relationship between Jesus and the Father (John 17:21). Every event He allows into your life is designed to make you more like Christ.

God's call came when He invited you to join Him on the journey! His call was extremely personal, designed specifically for your response. How wonderful to realise that, at a particular moment in history, Almighty God spoke personally to you and invited you to become His child!

What could possibly be stopping you from realising your destiny with God? Because of sin, we can never live blamelessly until He returns, but God has promised to forgive our sins and declare us justified. (1 John 1:9.) Now He invites you to join Him in working out His will in your life.

If, like I did at the airport, you have become distracted – or if you feel you are presently on a different path to what God intends for you – there is hope. Even if you find yourself on a detour, it does not mean God has changed His mind about your destination.

As you will see from the rest of my story, God has a way to get us back on the right track.

Let God lead

After about three hours on this new plane, headed towards a new destination, I finally got around to praying. I felt I had let God down and had taken my eye off the goal. I asked the flight hostess how much it would cost to get to Kennedy Airport from LaGuardia. She told me, 'It's gonna cost you around US $180 to get a taxi to get you there in time.'

There were three problems on my mind that had to be solved. My luggage and hand luggage: would they be safe? My money and the tickets for my connecting flight were in my hand luggage. Then there was the question of the connecting flight. It was scheduled to leave from Kennedy for London at 8pm that evening. The plane I was on would arrive at LaGuardia for 6.30pm.

'It's about an hour's drive from LaGuardia to

Kennedy', the hostess added.

'It's gonna be very tight, but you may just get there in time.'

Great! I thought, *Another adrenaline-pumping, roller-coaster journey!*

My main concern, however, was that I had been told it would cost me $180 while all I had with me was $10. Despite all the turmoil and disappointment, I knew that I had to reach out to God and seek His help to get me out of this mess. During the first three hours of the flight I had my head in my hands, spoke to no one, and refused to eat any food. I was so discouraged. I was not surprised when the man sitting next to me took the advantage of moving to a vacant seat three rows ahead. It was time to stop feeling sorry for myself and to pray, even if I didn't feel like it. How important that thought was to be for me throughout the rest of my Christian journey. How many times I have found myself praying when everything within me didn't want to – and yet I knew that was what I needed to do.

My prayer was simple, but heart-felt. I asked God to forgive me for being distracted and allowing the attractions around me to cloud my mind. I asked Him to help me in the three concerns that were on my mind and to get me back on the track to my original destination. I also asked God to give me a sign that He would be with me.

After praying, I remember putting my hand in my pocket and taking out the $10. I sat back in the chair and straightened out the crumpled note, and held it in the air and began to stare at the print. Then suddenly I saw something on that dollar bill which I had never noticed before in the whole year that I had been using US currency. My eyes came into focus on four words which are written on all $10 bills. The words were, 'IN GOD WE TRUST'. That was my sign! I smiled broadly to myself, took a long, deep sigh, nodded my head in amazement and thought, *Wow, Lord, you really are awesome!*

His ways are not our ways

I didn't know how God was going to work it out, but I was fully assured that He was going to do something miraculous!

At last my mind was at peace. The words of Isaiah 26:3 are so true: 'You will keep him in perfect peace, Whose mind is stayed on You, Because he trusts in You.' (NKJV.)

I relaxed for the rest of the flight, and asked the flight hostess for the food I'd missed and the drinks that passed by. I knew that God was going to sort it all out.

When I arrived in LaGuardia, the first place I headed for was where the taxis were. Knowing that I needed the rest of the money, I was constantly looking around on the floor. Maybe I would find a bundle of money, or perhaps bump into a long-lost relative or friend. I wasn't sure how God would do it, but I knew He would. I asked directions to the taxi stands and headed straight there. When I arrived, to my utter relief there was a hand-written sign by the side of the road saying:

'Today only, special shuttle taxi service to Kennedy Airport, for only $7.'

I was totally amazed. I had been thinking that somehow this money would 'fall from the sky' when all the time God was planning that I should use exactly what I already had – $10 – leaving me with enough change to buy myself a drink!

Our extremity is God's opportunity. He knows how to use what is already at our disposal to bring about His desired will. Proverbs 3:5, 6 (NKJV) tells us to:

'Trust in the LORD with all your heart, And lean not on your own understanding; In all your ways acknowledge Him, And He shall direct your paths.'

I was now on the shuttle taxi headed to Kennedy Airport. I was moving a little closer toward my original destination. However, there were two other things that now began to trouble my mind.

It's in times when we experience God's provision and mighty working that our adversary in life, the one who seeks to take us off the right track, will come in and try to discourage us. Having just seen God work in a marvellous way, suddenly the negative thoughts began to reappear. *So what about your luggage? You'll never catch your connecting flight in just forty-five minutes!* Once again I leaned towards becoming quite anxious, especially as this taxi seemed to be travelling at 20 miles per hour!

Listen to His voice

The truth is, the Christian race in life is not run on flat terrain. It's not always on a one-lane level. As we shall discover later, we do have to go through our mountaintop experiences, as well as those times in the valley of despondency. Despite the 'ups and downs', the questions we need to keep asking ourselves are these: 'Am I travelling on the right track?' and 'Am I still heading closer to my destination?'

When I finally arrived at Kennedy Airport, I went straight to the airline's lost baggage department. I explained to the attendant what had happened and she asked,

'Do you have ID tags to identify the bags?'

I explained that they were attached to my tickets in my hand luggage, which was left on the plane.

'Well, with no ID tags your bags could be anywhere!' she responded, rather unmercifully.

She showed me a large storeroom filled with hundreds of 'ownerless' bags and said, 'If your bag's lost, it will be in there somewhere.' I was left alone in the warehouse of lost bags: where would I begin? I said a simple prayer:

'Lord, please help me find my bags; show me the way.'

I knew what I was looking for, and, feeling impressed to start on the bags on the near left-hand side, my eyes began to scan like a radar, until within just a few moments I saw my two blue, battered suitcases and my small black hand luggage. I opened the bag and, with a sigh of relief, noticed that all my money was still there, my passport was there and my connecting tickets were all intact. Nothing was missing.

There are times in the Christian journey when we will stand at the crossroads: times when we will need to choose a direction in life from among a number of diverging paths, and say, 'Lord, which path do you want me to take?' If we just keep still long enough to listen to God's still, small voice, we will hear Him say, 'This is the way, walk ye in it' (Isaiah 30:21, KJV).

I have learned since that day that God always speaks to us. Sometimes we are just too busy to hear Him. We crowd our minds with so much noise. If it's not the TV, it's the computer, the iPod, the car radio or our mobile phones.

It seems that something always has to entertain our minds. Is it any wonder that we fail to discern God's voice and end up making wrong choices? Many of us are simply not 'tuned in' to Him – and then we accuse God of not listening to us and abandoning us in our problems.

It gets brighter along the way

The Bible states, in Proverbs 4:18 (KJV), 'But the path of the just is as the shining light, that shineth more and more unto the perfect day.'

You see, God wants you to walk by faith – to trust Him. The future may look dark and you may not know how you are going to get to that divine destination, but you will trust God, and take the next step that you know: stay close to God and abide in Him. The path lights up as you travel along it, and it shines brighter and brighter. When you are walking according to God's plan and purpose it will surely lead to a positive end!

You don't need to get stressed out trying to figure out how to make your life work; you don't need to manipulate or force things to happen; and you will learn to be satisfied with where you are in life, knowing that you will get to that final destination.

Well, by now, with suitcases in hand, and almost

satisfied that at least two of my three requests were answered, I made my way to the check-in desk to reschedule my flight. My plane was scheduled for 8pm, and, with all the drama in getting to the airport and finding the luggage, the time had lapsed – it was now 9pm. Knowing that I would have to stay overnight at a hotel, my thoughts were about where I would go and how much it would cost.

I went to the check-in desk and said to the attendant, 'My name is Richard Daly, and I was scheduled for the 8pm flight to London.'

I was about to explain why I was late and had missed the flight, when the lady at the check-in desk responded, 'Oh, didn't you hear the announcement?'

'What announcement?' I replied, wondering what could possibly happen now.

'The flight that was scheduled for 8pm has been delayed for three hours. You have an hour before we check in!'

You should have seen my face. With jaw dropped wide open and eyes bulging, I lifted my head heavenward and shouted, 'Thank You!'

I don't think the check-in lady had ever received such a positive exclamation at the announcement of a plane delay!

Well, God truly came through for me that day. I actually had one hour for myself. You can be fully assured that I did not wander off anywhere in that airport. In fact, I stayed put, right there! My lesson had been learnt.

In reflection, I often think about this experience and the wonderful promise given to us – that '. . . all things work together for good to those who love God, to those who are the called according to His purpose.' (Romans 8:28, NKJV.)

Begin the journey

As I mentioned before, we are all called according to His purpose. We are all invited to join in the Christian race. He assures us that this Christian race is '. . . not to the swift, nor the battle to the strong' (Ecclesiastes 9:11, KJV).

Today, Christ's invitation for each one of us is to begin this journey with Him: to embark with Him on an exciting race along a path of life that can bring us a greater sense of self-worth and assurance; discovering who we really are in Christ and how much we are loved and valued in the eyes of God. It is a journey of self-discovery. But it's more than that. It is taking the attention away from ourselves for a while, and recognising that there is a Supreme Being who is all-mighty, glorious and powerful, and who is in control of the universe. This same God is also very personal. He is as close as we will allow Him to be. His attention to the details of our lives, His care and consideration to our every concern, reveals One who wants to truly know us and, in return, for us to discover who He really is.

So, finally, there I was on the original plane I ought to have been on in the first place, headed toward my original destination. I was finally on my way home.

I encourage you to accept God's destination for your life. Get on board with Christ, and let the journey begin. Why not seal your decision by completing the response below?

Your personal response

I believe Jesus Christ is the son of the Living God. I want Him to be the Lord of my life and for Him to plan my journey for me.

Signed: _____

Date: _____

chapter two

Run to win

One of the most memorable sports days I had at college was when I ran the 400 metres. Not only was I to run the most gruelling race, a flat-out sprint once round the track, but I also had to face the 'mean machine'! That's what we called him. He stood about 6 feet 3 inches tall; was solid and muscular all over; and had a bald head and the most intimidating presence about him. His name was Basil Been.

I knew that, if I were to stand any chance of being near him in the race, I had to train – and train very hard! With just four weeks until sports day I 'took to the track' and tried to regain some of my running form from two years earlier!

In order to assist in my preparations, I called upon a good friend of mine, Delroy Foster. He knew a bit about running techniques and training routines. I was glad to have him around because, no matter how poorly I performed, he always saw ways in which I could improve.

So each week, from Monday to Friday during lunch-times, we trained in three 300-metre laps followed by two 400-metre laps, then one of 500 metres, with only fifteen minutes of rest in between. Needless to say, it was gruelling!

'No matter what, Richard,' he advised during one of our fifteen-minute breaks, 'when you are headed down the final stretch, you must always, always keep your eyes on that finishing line; never look back!'

Sometimes the training would be so intense that I was only too glad to see that finish line! However, I always appreciated his words of advice. . . .

'Remember to run your own race; set a steady pace and keep focused!' he would always say.

With all the training and hard workouts, in no time the four weeks had elapsed, and sports day was upon me.

I've always enjoyed track and field events, and that's probably why I volunteered to become a chaplain at the Sydney Olympic Games in 2000. Combining my love for sports and my vocation as a clergyman seemed the perfect arrangement. It was also an opportunity to witness many sporting achievements, as well as the brave attempts of

Olympians to perform at their best. I will never forget the final of the women's 400-metre race which included the Australian athlete, Cathy Freeman. Just a few days before, she represented her entire nation by lighting the Olympic torch at the opening ceremony, a feat usually performed by some past Olympic legend. What pressure that must have been for her, knowing she probably had a lot still to prove.

Yet, as I watched from the stands, Cathy Freeman, who was wearing her all-in-one green body-suit and hood to match, rose to the occasion. With almost everyone in the packed 70,000-seat stadium standing, cheering and roaring her on, Cathy 'did the business'. As if going into an extra gear, she stormed home in the last 50 metres, beating her rivals to take first place. What a victory! I don't think anyone in the crowd failed to salute her.

Cathy ran to win, and win she did!

I knew that, if I was going to beat Basil Been, I also had to run to win. We lined up on our blocks. I had been drawn on the outside lane, with Been on the inside lane just behind me. The gun fired and we were off. I quickly got into my stride, and maintained a fast, steady speed. I was always conscious that Been was nearby. What made things a little more challenging was that once he got into his stride he had a habit of breathing quite loudly through his mouth, making a loud 'whooooing' sound in the process. At first it was quite intimidating, but after a while it helped me gauge exactly where he was in the race.

We came round to the last bend, with just 80 metres to go. To my surprise, when all lanes had levelled out, I was in the lead. By now the lactic acid began building up in my legs, and my head got lighter and fuzzier as I gasped deeper for air. *Can I make it to the finish and win this race?* I thought. What now concerned me was that I could no longer hear Been breathing behind me. Where was he? How much more energy did I need to exert to beat him? How much of a last push? I just wanted to know where he was!

I was tempted to just glance to my left to see if he was there. With just 15 metres to go, it was tiring, and I was slowing down. I was about to look back when, amid all the cheering and noise, I heard a very distinctive voice. It was my friend Delroy Foster shouting at the top of his voice: 'Come on, Richard. Come on, Richard. You can do it! Keep your eyes on the line!'

His familiar voice seemed like an extra boost of adrenaline. I remembered his words, 'Always keep focused; keep your eyes on the finishing line and never look back.'

With those words of encouragement, I gave one last surge without looking back and crossed that finishing line first, beating the formidable Basil Been. It turned out that I had won by one hundredth of a second. If I had glanced back, I would have lost the race. Fortunately, I remained focused – and won.

The ancient games

The Olympic Games, as we know them today, have a long history which goes back to ancient times.

Sports competitions were organised at Olympia and were named after their location: hence the name, 'Olympic Games'. Nobody knows exactly when they began, but the date of 776 BC is often referred to as the first written mention of the competitions.

These games were held at the same place, every four years.

They were organised at Olympia and led to the development of the Panhellenic Games. These included:

- *The games at Olympia (Olympic Games)*
- *The games at Delphi (Pythian Games)*
- *The games at Isthmia (Isthmian Games)*
- *The games at Nemea (Nemean Games).*

An Olympic victor was crowned with an olive wreath and had his name inscribed in the official Olympic records. Olympic victors were considered as heroes and conferred honour upon their city-states.

During the lifetime of the apostle Paul, the ancient

games in Olympia, Greece, would have been in full swing. His writing in particular contains many words and phrases concerning the games of biblical times, because they were household terms that powerfully communicated God's truths by comparing the known and familiar terms of the Olympic Games to the spiritual truths of God's Word. An example of this can be seen in 1 Corinthians 9:24-27. These verses of Scripture have more Olympic terminology than any other passage:

'Do you not know that those who run in a race all run, but only one receives the prize? Run in such a way that you may win.' (1 Corinthians 9:24, NASB.)

Paul makes the call for us to be winners in the Christian race. This call is not about being first, but about staying in the race until the end.

You can run the first part of the race in record time, but it won't mean anything if you never cross the finish line.

It is on this basis that Paul gives the believers at Corinth an exhortation. It is not just an exhortation to participate in the race, but to run so that they will win.

Run in such a way

Winning the spiritual race doesn't depend upon how fast you can run; instead, it is determined by how you run.

Ecclesiastes 9:11 says:

'... The race is not to the swift or the battle to the strong, nor does food come to the wise or wealth to the brilliant or favor to the learned; but time and chance happen to them all' (NIV).

From God's perspective, winning is not based upon speed, strength, intelligence or wealth.

In the view of many, people are successful if they are the best – number one or top of the class. But God is more concerned with us doing our best to honour Him. Therefore, from God's standpoint, winning is based upon our willingness and desire to please Him, and to live our lives in harmony with His will.

The advantage that the Christian has over the athlete is that only one athlete in any given sport may win the first prize. The athlete has only human assistance in the form of trainers and coaches. Every Christian, however, has the opportunity to be a winner, for there are no second-place runners. In the Christian race, each runner needs to complete the race to be acknowledged by God as a winner. We should understand that in this race the Christian is not competing against other Christians. We all have the same access to the power of Jesus Christ through the agency of the Holy Spirit. With Jesus, there is no losing for the Christian, but without Jesus there would be no victory.

The Christian Race

Paul says we should run 'in such a way' as to win. Among the many parallels that can be gleaned from the athlete, we can also learn from the approach winners have toward their sport.

In the ancient games there was a qualification for selection – the rule of birth. The athlete needed to be a bona fide citizen, born and bred in the country he wished to represent, before he could be allowed to run. In the Christian race, we must be born again before we can qualify to run.

The athletes needed to have practised and prepared according to the rules before they could participate in the race. In taking part in the Christian race, we need to live according to moral rules spelt out in God's Word.

There was a need for the athletes to keep on the running track, or else they were disqualified; similarly, the Christian also needs to keep on the path that leads to God's final destination for us.

The athletes were required to be free from stimulants, hard drugs and substance abuse. In the same way, the Christians running the Christian race are to recognise that their bodies are the temple of God, the dwelling place of the Holy Spirit (1 Corinthians 6:19).

The athletes were determined, right from the start, to run the race to the end – come what may. Christians likewise are exhorted to 'endure to the end' (Matthew 24:13).

Who are winners?

Tom Venuto, in his article, 'What It Takes to Be a Champion',[1] lists (among others) eleven qualities of a champion. The spiritual parallels are quite interesting.

=1= Winners are positive thinkers.

Undoubtedly the most important quality that all champions share is an unwavering belief that they will succeed. Champions always look for the good in every situation. No matter what obstacles they encounter, they continue to think positive thoughts. Proverbs tells us, 'For as he thinketh in his heart, so is he' (Proverbs 23:7, KJV). It is your thoughts, not your circumstances, that determine your attitude. Daniel was a winner because he '. . . purposed in his heart that he would not defile himself' (Daniel 1:8, KJV) with the king's food. We must believe the promise that Jesus gave: '. . . With men this is impossible; but with God all things are possible' (Matthew 19:26, KJV).

=2= Winners visualise their successes.

Winners understand the importance of positive mental imagery, or visualisation. They mentally rehearse winning every race in vivid detail. They do this over and over in their minds, hundreds or even thousands of times, before it becomes a physical reality.

Job was a winner. He visualised the change that would happen one day in his life: '. . . I will wait, Till my change comes' (Job 14:14, NKJV). Abraham '. . . looked for a city which hath foundations, whose builder and maker is God' (Hebrews 11:10, KJV). These men had faith, which is seeing and claiming the finished product before it arrives.

=3= Winners surround themselves with positive people and avoid negative influences.

Champions keep themselves in a positive mode and do not associate with negative people, places, or things. We as Christians are exhorted, in the race, to '. . . lay aside every weight, and the sin which so easily ensnares us' (Hebrews 12:1, NKJV); to 'Turn not to the right hand nor to the left: remove thy foot from evil' (Proverbs 4:27, KJV). With Christ as our Supreme Example, when we surround ourselves with Him we become fortified and mentally renewed to face life's challenges.

=4= Winners are goal-setters.

Winners realise that, if they don't know where they're going, that is exactly where they'll end up – nowhere! Champions consistently set long- and short-term goals. From day-to-day workout goals to long-term career objectives, champions have specific, written, measurable goals, each with a deadline.

This ought to be the same with us. We are told that if we commit our plans to the Lord, trusting in Him, He shall bring them to pass (Psalm 37:5 and Proverbs 16:3). Allowing the Lord to guide our steps and direct our paths as we seek Him becomes the first premise upon which our goals and aspirations are based.

=**5**= *Winners have a burning desire to succeed.*

Champions not only have goals, but they ardently desire to achieve them. They have a burning desire to excel. That's why Paul says we must not only run the race, but 'run to win'. It ought to be a joy to want to serve God and to do His will. One of the most beautiful promises of Scripture says, 'Delight yourself in the LORD and he will give you the desires of your heart' (Psalm 37:4, NIV). This promise will be met on the condition that we have a genuine, sincere desire to 'delight ourselves' in the Lord. God wants us to succeed in all areas of our lives – our studies, work, relationships and finance – but most of all our spiritual lives. It is when you '. . . seek first the kingdom of God and His righteousness' that everything else 'shall be added to you.' (Matthew 6:33, NKJV.)

The Christian Race

=6= Winners are disciplined and consistent.

Winners are committed and disciplined in training and dietary practices. They know that in their sport there is no off-season, and that success does not come overnight. They are dedicated to their chosen sport.

Paul takes this quality of an athlete and, in applying it to himself, says: 'Therefore I run thus: not with uncertainty. Thus I fight: not as one who beats the air. But I discipline my body and bring it into subjection . . .' (1 Corinthians 9:26, 27, NKJV).

Every winner seeks to live a disciplined life. As Christians, we must recognise that our lives are governed by higher principles of behaviour and moral conduct. A Christian is a follower of Christ. We live according to His teachings and truths, found in the Word of God. The Bible is our training manual, and we too must live consistently, for we can have no 'off seasons'. We are called to be faithful even unto death, and the reward will be a crown of life (Revelation 2:10).

=7= Winners learn from their failures.

Champions don't view losses as failures; they see them as learning experiences. Thomas Edison was the epitome of persistence: he conducted 10,000 experiments before finally finding a filament that would burn in the electric light bulb. Winners approach their vocation with the same diligence as Edison. They know that, if they persist long enough, eventually they must succeed. When asked how it felt to fail 10,000 times, Thomas Edison replied, 'I didn't fail; I learned 9,999 ways that wouldn't work.' Winners know that they haven't failed until they quit; but once they quit, then they have failed. A true winner finds a lesson in every apparent loss, and finds ways to grow from it.

The Christian path is full of hurdles and pitfalls which can make us fall. Distractions keep us off the right path, but the committed Christian, though he may stumble and fall, will not stay down. The assurance is given, 'Many are the afflictions of the righteous, But the LORD delivers him out of them all' (Psalm 34:19, NKJV). The prophet Micah says, 'When I fall, I will arise; When I sit in darkness, The LORD will be a light to me.' (Micah 7:8, NKJV.) Let us learn from our mistakes and failures to enable us to become stronger. Remember you have one Person on your side who is 'able to keep you from falling' (Jude 24, KJV).

=*8*= Winners have a deep love and boundless enthusiasm for their sport.

To a loser, training and dieting are work and drudgery. To a champion, training and dieting are labours of love, a joy and a passion. Champions are enthusiastic about what they do; they can't wait to train each day. Motivational speaker Tom Hopkins once said, 'Work is anything you're doing when you'd rather be doing something else.' Champions are doing what they love, so to them it's not work at all; it's fun!

The Christian path ought to be the one on which we love to be. Our relationship with Christ should be based on a personal zeal and joy, knowing that our sins have been forgiven; that we have been saved from eternal destruction; and that we have been given a new destination. The fact that Christ died for you and changed your life, giving you renewed hope and loving you without limit, ought to be the primary reason why you want to serve Him. Our Christian life should not be laborious and full of drudgery, but ought to be lived with an enthusiastic delight.

=*9*= Winners strive for constant improvement.

Winners are never satisfied with the status quo; they never rest on their laurels. They aim for small improvements, every day in every way. Champions are always looking for a better way to do things. Although winners are always striving for more, they also realise that success is a journey, so they enjoy each moment and savour every step along the way.

Paul expressed this characteristic of a winner when he said, '. . . forgetting those things which are behind

and reaching forward to those things which are ahead,
I press toward the goal' (Philippians 3:13, 14, NKJV,
emphasis supplied). 'Pressing forward' means 'to
make progress'. 'Running to win' means to '. . . grow
in the grace and knowledge of our Lord and Savior
Jesus Christ.' (2 Peter 3:18, NKJV.)

Paul also says, in Philippians 3:12, 'Not that I have
already obtained all this, or have already been made
perfect, but I press on to take hold of that for which
Christ Jesus took hold of me' (NIV).

The apostle Paul states in no uncertain terms that
he had not become perfect in this life (vs.12). He
readily admitted that he was far from perfection. He
even referred to himself as the 'chief of sinners' (1
Timothy 1:15). However, Paul didn't give up when he
realised that he couldn't attain perfection in this life! In
Philippians 3, verses 12 to 14, he tells us that he was
continuing to press forward and that he was expecting
to make progress. He was looking forward to the time
when he would become perfect, but that time would
come in the future when he would be with the Lord. In
fact, finally reaching the state of perfection and being
fully conformed to the image of Christ was to be part
of the prize upon reaching Heaven (vs.14). There can
be, and should be, moral progress in this life now –
but moral perfection will not come until later.

=10= Winners are willing to go the extra mile.

Positive thinking, goal-setting, visualisation, desire, persistence and enthusiasm are vital, but without action and hard work these traits are all worthless. Champions are hard workers. They take consistent action and they are willing to do the things losers are not prepared to do. Champions make themselves go to the gym when they don't feel like going. They stay on the bike another fifteen minutes, even when they are exhausted. They do five extra reps after others have stopped. Champions are steadfast with their diets when others break down and cheat. Champions have the willingness to train through the pain barrier while the 'non-champions' quit when it starts to hurt. In short, champions go the extra mile.

The Christian who runs to win will realise that salvation lies not in works but only through faith, which is manifested, or made evident, in works. Therefore he is challenged to go the extra mile by stretching his faith beyond his comfort zone. Going the extra mile involves praying when we don't feel like it, and spending time in the Word of God when the initial desire is not there. It is doing what Jesus asked us to do when He said in Matthew 5:41: '. . . whoever compels you to go one mile, go with him two.' (NKJV.) This verse follows the passage about 'turning the other cheek'. Jesus reorders all human relationships. He wants us to ask, 'How can I be a redemptive blessing even toward those who mistreat me?' His challenging commands awaken us to our responsibility. We are to go the extra mile and lead others to Jesus – even those whom we don't particularly like.

These are some of the qualities of a winner. Yet, like me racing against Basil Been, we can be assured that the enemy will be breathing down our backs to bring fear and uncertainty. It's during these moments that we hear a voice like Delroy Foster, reminding us not to turn back but to keep our eyes on the goal. If there were to be one more quality of a winner, it would be the ability to keep focused.

=11= Winners have the ability to remain focused.

Back in 1954, Roger Bannister had held the world record for running the mile for just six weeks until his great rival, John Landy of Australia, broke it by more than a second with a time of 3:58.0. The stage was now set for a dramatic showdown between the two runners in the final of the One Mile at the Empire Games in Vancouver.

This race was probably the most exciting mile race ever run, and is still known as the 'Miracle Mile'. A statue stands in Vancouver to commemorate its moment of highest drama, when John Landy looked back over his left shoulder just as Roger Bannister passed him on his right. About that moment Landy said: 'When Lot's wife looked back she was turned into a pillar of salt. When I looked back I was turned into a pillar of bronze!'

Fix your eyes

Paul takes up this theme when he says, '. . . let us run with perseverance the race marked out for us. Let us fix our eyes on Jesus, the author and perfecter of our faith' (Hebrews 12:1, 2, NIV).

We are called to fix our eyes on Jesus. The word 'fix' comes from a Greek word that has the idea of concentrating your gaze. It means to look away from other things so that you can focus all your attention on one object.

There is no one more beautiful to fix your eyes upon than Jesus. Let us fix our eyes on His ultimate sacrifice for our sins on the cross of Calvary; fix our eyes upon His glorious resurrection; fix our eyes upon Jesus to be saved, healed, delivered and set free. This was exactly what Peter did.

In Matthew 14 we read of the miracle of Jesus walking on water. What a sight it must have been for the disciples. When Peter called out to Jesus, he was the only person on the boat who reacted to Jesus in faith. Peter said to Jesus, 'Lord, if it's you, tell me to come to you on the water.' Walking on water was an impossible task for Peter – but, instead of focusing on the improbability of his success, he focused on Jesus. Basically, Peter was saying that, even though the task seemed impossible, he would try it if it was Jesus' will.

Jesus' reply to this request was a simple one. He did not need a long dissertation to explain to Peter how to walk on water or to explain the physics behind it or anything else. Jesus simply replied to Peter's request with one word – 'Come'.

This is how it should work within the Christian race. When faced with impossible choices or conditions, we should look to Jesus and ask Him what His will is for us. Does He want us to step out in faith, or cower in the boat? More often than not, His response will be for us to 'Come'. We may not always be comfortable. We might not always be doing exactly what we want to do. But, if we truly follow His guidance and live by His will, we will have to step out of that boat and walk with Him in faith.

When Peter stepped out of the boat, initially he was fine. He was actually doing the impossible and walking on water, because it was Jesus' will for him. It was only when Peter took his eyes off Jesus and noticed the wind and the waves, and began focusing on the impossibility of his task, that he started to sink.

It is not enough for us to step out in faith. We have

to keep our eyes on Jesus. We can't start focusing on how hard it is, or on any storms that may pop up along the way. If we do that we will start to sink and fall into despair. If we keep our eyes on Jesus and have complete faith in Him to make His will happen, we will not sink. We will continue to walk with Him on the water.

However, even if we find ourselves sinking, we can take another lesson from Peter. When he began to sink, he did not try to save himself. He did the only thing he could possibly do in that situation – he reached out to Jesus. His cry was, 'Lord, save me.' As humans we sometimes have a tendency to try to fix everything ourselves. But Jesus is the real Answer. He is the real Solution. If we find ourselves sinking, we must reach out to Him for help. Instead of pulling away when we start to sink, it is at those times that we must draw closer to Him. Just as He did with Peter, Jesus will save us in those circumstances.

I constantly remind myself to step off that boat and walk in faith. I remind myself to do His will – not mine. And I remind myself to keep my eyes on Jesus. He is the way and the truth and the life.

Jesus wants us to be winners in the Christian race. We must 'stand firm' and stay true to the One who can deliver us from anything that tries to distract us or drown us in sin and keep us from the right path. We

should always hold onto Jesus in the storms of life,
and never let go. Storms will come and go, but we will
be safe and secure when we keep our eyes on Jesus.

[1] *http://www.articlestop10.com/what-takes-champ.php*

chapter three

The disciplined training
Becoming better equipped to run effectively

The thought of running 26 miles had never really impressed me. I always like to see the finishing line before I start a race. Yet every time I watched the London Marathon on TV I was always moved by the commitment and endurance of the runners. It is an inspiration. So much so that in the year 2000 I decided I would apply to run – but I was not going to do it alone. Larry was going to run with me.

When I approached him about the idea, I was none too surprised by his response.

'You must be out of your mind! I can just about run from the house to my car opposite the gate', he continued, laughing it off. 'What thought possessed you to want to do this, let alone to come here and even associate my name with all of this?' he enquired rather inquisitively.

'Larry, we can do it!' I said, looking him straight in

the eyes. 'If we start training now, we have seven months before April. That's enough time to get into shape – besides, think of the weight you're going to lose just training! It's a real challenge! And I know you love challenges.' Larry began to look shocked as he realised I was serious about this. 'See it as a personal goal, and just think – you will be able to tell everyone that in the year 2000, at the start of a new millennium, you ran the London Marathon. That will be forever immortalised in your life's legacy, and you can tell your children, your grandchildren, your. . . .'

'Wait a minute!' Larry interjected, knowing that I was on a roll, and with a large sigh began to ask detailed questions. 'So who can apply? How many miles is this? How many days, I mean hours, will it take?'

I outlined all the information: the training schedules, timelines, possible charity organisations we could run for; even down to the type of trainers we should buy. It was a hard task, but I finally convinced Larry, my uncle of 75 years of age, to run the London Marathon with me!

There are many sporting achievements by individuals who defied all the odds to succeed, regardless of age, experience, health or social conditions. Such individuals may not have come first or broken national records, but neither were they fazed or intimidated by other competitors.

The Christian Race

I think of Eric Moussambani, from Equatorial Guinea. He learned to swim in January when his nation established its first aquatics federation. Seven months later, he stepped onto his blocks in baggy blue trunks to make his Olympic debut at Sydney in the 100-metre freestyle.

He had only ever raced over 50 metres before in a 20-metre-long pool, and the Olympic waters of the Sydney International Aquatic Centre stretched out before him like a marathon course.

The starter called the swimmers to their marks. Moussambani, 5 feet 7 inches, held steady.

The gun fired – Eric the Eel, as he would later be called, plunged into the lane and eventually ended last in a time of 1 minute, 52.72 seconds.

Ian Thorpe had raced to a silver medal in 1 minute 45 seconds over double the distance the day before.

The largely Australian crowd – nearly every man, woman and child probably capable of swimming faster than Moussambani – warmed to the occasion.

His was a moment of true inspiration and courage in a given task. He never allowed his shortcomings to hinder him.

That's how God wants us to think about how we approach our spiritual journey with Him. He accepts us just as we are. Regardless of our failures and weaknesses, God sees something in you and me of such great worth and value that He was prepared to put His life on the line for it.

How Christ views you is of much more importance than how others do, or even how you view yourself. Christ sees your potential; He sees your destiny and knows what you can become when you are prepared to put your implicit trust in Him. He takes us at our point of entry, and begins a work of reformation and change that is character-transforming. As the potter with the clay, he moulds and shapes us until we become objects of greater beauty.

According to the Olympic motto, 'The most important thing in the Olympic Games is not to win but to take part'. The same is true for the most important thing in our spiritual journey with Jesus – the decision to take part. It's not about being first or last, but staying the course, which will ultimately cause you to become a winner.

After much thought and agonising contemplation, Uncle Larry finally decided that he would run the London Marathon. This meant we both had to engage in serious training. Neither one of us had really run more than 3 miles in one go, so to prepare for 26 meant not just a rigorous physical schedule, but to somehow develop a mental self-belief that we could do this. For Uncle Larry this would become perhaps the most single challenging task of his life. Would his body of 75 years of age still have the 'staying power' to keep him going?

As time went by, Uncle Larry stuck to his programme of training. His confidence increased, as well as his motivation and zeal. Three-mile morning runs turned into 5 miles, then 8. Being more agile and fitter than Uncle Larry, my schedule was a bit more intense. I found I was trying to fit in too much in a shorter period of time. Before too long, my body responded with sudden pains in my right knee – the recurrence of a former injury. Every time I reached the 3-mile mark my knee did not want any more of it, and signalled that to me with shooting pains. I knew it was not going to work. My dream of running the London Marathon was over before I had even started.

I wondered if Uncle Larry would still want to run without me, seeing that I was the one who persuaded him in the first place. To my joy, Uncle Larry responded quite defiantly: 'I've started the training, so I might as well go all the way.'

The apostle Paul, during his missionary travels, would no doubt see athletes in training for the games. Maybe that's why he mentions in 1 Corinthians 9:25 (NIV):

'Everyone who competes in the games goes into strict training. They do it to get a crown that will not last; but we do it to get a crown that will last forever. . . . I beat my body and make it my slave. . . .'

Any Olympic athlete will tell you that to get to one race in the Olympics takes four years of training. Usain Bolt, the 100-metre and 200-metre world and Olympic champion, as well as world record holder, described his strenuous daily training schedule, under the strict discipline of his coach, as waking up at 5.30am each morning to 'Judgement Day'. Yet such is the regime of successful athletes. Those who want to perform at their best are prepared to make sacrifices, spend countless hours working on their technique, subjecting their bodies to the limit in order to shave a few hundredths of a second off their personal best or a few millimetres off their distance.

The Christian journey with Christ likewise calls for training and discipline. We have to spend time and energy training ourselves for spiritual fitness. The apostle Paul calls it 'training in godliness' (1 Timothy 4:8). What makes something a spiritual discipline is taking that specific part of your life and turning it towards God. A spiritual discipline is something that, when practised faithfully and regularly as a pattern in your life, repeatedly brings you back to God and opens you up to what God is saying to you.

Here are a few of the prominent spiritual disciplines:

Prayer

John Calvin was fond of saying, 'Prayer is the chief

exercise of faith.'

Jesus gave a clear example of how to exercise prayer. He prayed, and prayed, and prayed some more. He prayed in marathon sessions before major developments in his life (for example, the calling of the twelve, and His crucifixion). He prayed with others in public in the synagogue, where He worshipped every Sabbath. He prayed alone on countless occasions. The Gospels depict Him going away to a lonely place a great while before day in order to be alone and to pray. What Jesus knew to be essential we can't allow to be optional. Since prayer is the chief exercise of faith, believing people are equipped chiefly through prayer. Apart from it, Christ Himself would plainly have had no ministry. We cannot do without the very thing that He knew to be His lifeline.

Meditation on Scripture

We experience God when we meditate on Scripture. Christian meditation on Scripture is an encounter with God through His written Word. This discipline bears no resemblance to the practice of meditation in the eastern religions.

When we meditate on Scripture, our minds interact with the Bible. We read or listen to a passage and ponder over what God wants it to tell us. Either a single verse or an entire section is appropriate. We simply sit in silence and allow God's Word to pour over us and wash through our hearts. In a sense, meditation on Scripture is our dress rehearsal as we attempt to live out the Word that God writes on our hearts. He transforms us and restores us to reflect His image.

Meditation on Scripture cultivates our sensitivity to the still, small voice of God. His Word comes alive through dialogue in this discipline. As we ponder the Scriptures, we may see a vision or receive interpretations and insights that are very personal. We intentionally set our personal thoughts to one side so that we can receive what God has for us from His written Word.

Meditation on Scripture is a vital source of spiritual nourishment for all Christians. Reading and studying the Bible is important. But meditating on the Word of God transforms the information we store in our brains into God's personal work in our hearts.

Fasting

Fasting expresses our hunger for God. 'Why spend money on what is not bread, and your labour on what does not satisfy?' (Isaiah 55:2, NIV-UK.) Jesus, who is the Bread of Life, invites us to find all our satisfaction in Him alone. Fasting is giving up food in exchange for spiritual nourishment.

Whatever our convictions might be about fasting, there are distinct advantages to this discipline which are only experienced by those who practise it.

Fasting reveals what controls us. It is amazing how much I am affected by skipping even one or two meals. I notice it both mentally and physically. I then realise how much I am being controlled by the body, rather than by the Spirit. In this sense, fasting makes us aware of the need for balance, and for the need of 'Spirit aliveness' within us.

Fasting also increases the effectiveness of intercessory prayer. Fasting and prayer really go together. It brings an earnestness into the situation being prayed for, a seriousness that sharpens our concentration upon spiritual matters.

Sabbath rest

When we enter the Sabbath day of rest, we imitate God. 'By the seventh day God had finished the work he had been doing; so on the seventh day he rested from all his work.' (Genesis 2:2, NIV.) It's more than a commandment. It actually is part of God's created order. Plus, the Sabbath rest is for everyone, not just the Jews. As Jesus said, 'The Sabbath was made for man, not man for the Sabbath.' (Mark 2:27, NIV.)

Just as God rested on the seventh day, so we enter into His Sabbath rest by ending our week with activities that allow us to reflect, refresh ourselves and rest in Christ.

The discipline of Sabbath rest teaches us the rhythm of life that God established in creation. We intentionally choose to honour our Creator, not only by worshipping in a community of faith, but by following His example. Our non-stop busyness robs us of communion with Jesus. The writer of Hebrews said, 'There remains, then, a Sabbath-rest for the people of God; for anyone who enters God's rest also rests from his own work, just as God did from his. Let us, therefore, make every effort to enter that rest, so that no one will fall by following their example of disobedience.' (Hebrews 4:9-11, NIV.)

Solitude and contemplation

Contemplating God is one of the needful things that Jesus commends. Few people take time to be still and enjoy God's presence. But consider the Lord's instruction: 'Be still, and know that I am God' (Psalm 46:10, KJV). In the discipline of contemplation, we learn to be still and quiet the mind so that we can more fully comprehend the presence of the Lord.

The original and correct sense of the Greek verb 'to contemplate' is 'to behold'. We learn how to behold God through the practice of contemplation. In this spiritual discipline, we learn to be still in the body and quiet in the mind so that God can overwhelm us in the Spirit. Contemplation prepares us for a deeper experience of the divine presence of God.

The practice of contemplation as a spiritual discipline may seem a very simple thing to do, but it can be very difficult to master. These days, it is a challenge to be physically quiet and still, so it takes consistent discipline to silence even our thoughts. It's hard to hear the voice of God over the noise of our busy lives. We need to stop and be silent in order to hear Him. Why would you do all the talking during your prayer time, when God longs to whisper in your ear? Contemplate, behold God, and you will receive the gift of enjoying His divine presence.

Spiritual disciplines are not always easy to practise on a daily basis. In a true sense they are a battle between the spirit and the flesh. The spirit is willing, but the flesh is weak. However, disciplined living for the Christian means an intentional surrender to the superiority of the Spirit, leading to the lordship of Christ over all of your life.

Uncle Larry had now spent several months in training for the London Marathon. For a 75-year-old he had proved himself to be quite fit.

The day of the marathon finally arrived – and he was ready for it.

'I'll be cheering you on, Uncle Larry, from as many

points along the route as I can', I said, proudly. I was very excited for him.

As he wore a bright orange T-shirt with his name printed on the front and back, I marked him out in my mind, so that I could spot him among the thousands of runners.

At the 13-mile mark where I waited, I finally saw Uncle Larry from a distance. As he approached, I could see that so far he was in good shape: with a good, steady pace, buoyant and controlled. So far, so good. I don't think he noticed me at all, even though I shouted out his name. Uncle Larry seemed very focused on the task in hand.

My next stop was at the 20-mile mark.

I noticed that many runners at this stage were running quite laboriously. There were only 6 miles left, but many were resigned to walking the remaining miles; others were struggling at this stage. I wondered what condition Uncle Larry would be in once he passed here, because beyond this was unknown territory for him.

After he had been running for four and a half hours, I saw Uncle Larry in his bright orange T-shirt approaching. This time I could see that he was struggling. The stern expression on his face told me that he was in agony. By now his feet were shuffling as he plodded along, taking deep gasps of air. I feared that it was all a bit too much for him. Maybe I never briefed him enough on what could happen around this distance, a psychological and physical occurrence known as 'hitting the wall'.

It usually happens around mile 20, give or take a couple of miles. Your pace slows, sometimes considerably. Some runners say that it feels as though their legs have been filled with lead, and you can't feel your feet at all. The thought processes become a little fuzzy. Muscle co-ordination goes out of the window, and self-doubt casts a deep shadow over the soul.

Looking at Uncle Larry, I could see that he had all the symptoms of this experience.

In a similar way, these symptoms can also be evident in the Christian journey: the slowing down of spiritual fervour; zeal and enthusiasm beginning to wane; and self-doubt casting a deep shadow over the soul.

This may happen during a time of crisis when we may question God, or when – almost unexpectedly over a period of time – that first love experience with Christ loses its vitality.

We 'hit' that spiritual 'wall', where being a Christian becomes more of a struggle than a delight and joy. It may be a period of time when Christ no longer seems real to you. Maybe routine has set in and the journey has become rather mundane. There are times in my own spiritual journey when I go through periods like that. It's happened on more than one occasion – often when, for some reason, I have taken my eyes off the ball, neglected to spend time with God and thought that I still can get by on past spiritual experiences. It's when, in giving spiritually to others, I invariably have nothing more to give, because in helping to fill the wells of others I discover that my own has become dry and empty.

I remember listening to Phillips Idowu, Great Britain's triple jumper, being quizzed by reporters over his failure to win a medal at the world championships. He had been performing well all year long. His response was honest: 'I have neglected to keep doing what I had always been doing that won me medals. I thought I could still win just on the momentum.'

That is such a familiar experience. We can be found in a similar situation, thinking like myself that we can get by on the momentum of the past.

What is needed is a continual daily refreshing of God's blessing upon us, which is really only designed to get us through that day. Tomorrow calls for yet a further encounter. Jeremiah in his wisdom tells us:

'. . . His compassions fail not. They are new every morning; Great is Your faithfulness' (Lamentations 3:22, 23, NKJV).

Staying power to get through 'the wall' can be

achieved by a fresh revelation of who God is and what He can do for our lives on a daily basis. Spiritual disciplines, as outlined above – when practised on a daily basis – will prepare us for times when we hit that 'spiritual wall' of discouragement or challenging times.

I knew that if Uncle Larry was to get through, it would be dependent on how well he had trained. It was also dependent on how much he really wanted to complete the course.

This time I managed to get near to the finish line, and looked eagerly for him to appear. After five and a half hours of running, Uncle Larry finally appeared on the horizon among the blur of runners all heading towards the finishing line.

'Uncle Larry, you can do it! Keep going, keep going!' I shouted at the top of my voice.

I doubt if he heard, but somehow I knew that he was not going to give up at this stage.

This time he looked more at ease, his pace had picked up and there was hope in his eyes. He crossed the line triumphant. He did it. He broke through 'the wall' by sheer determination and on the strength gained from his training. He succeeded where many others had failed. He had completed the London Marathon, and I was deeply proud of him!

The next few hours were spent with him while he told me what it was like and how he felt.

'Do you know what kept me going?' he asked.

'What was it?' I asked, waiting for a moment of inspiring truth.

'The thought of you believing in me', he said with a smile – then he continued, 'When at times during that race I didn't believe in myself, I knew that you did.' I was greatly moved by those words. That was to be a defining moment for both of us.

chapter four

Jumping the hurdles
Avoiding the traps designed to make you fall

At the 2008 Beijing Olympic Games I had the opportunity of being an accredited Christian freelance journalist. I was looking for Christian athletes from around the world, for interviews and for opportunities to explore spiritual object lessons. The finals of the women's 100-metre hurdles was to prove to be a classic example of overcoming challenges within the spiritual realm.

The line-up involved the current world champion from the USA, Lolo Jones. She had been winning every race leading up to the Olympics, so she was the firm favourite to win.

Starting in lane 3, at the sound of the gun Lolo broke from the blocks a fraction too slow – but she was still in the race. A few hurdles into the race, her sprinter's speed kicked in, and she gradually closed on her competitors and surged to the lead.

As she neared the fateful ninth hurdle, she had established daylight between herself and the rest of the field. At that point, the only question appeared to be who would claim the silver and bronze medals.

But inside her head, Jones knew things were going awry.

'About the middle part of the race the hurdles were coming up very fast,' she said, 'and I just told myself what I always tell myself – keep things tight. I just could not maintain control. It's like you're racing a car and you're going as fast as you can and you hit a kerb and either you crash and burn or you maintain control. I crashed and burned today.'

After Jones hit the hurdle, she lurched back on her heels, eyes wide open as she desperately tried to maintain balance. She somehow managed to clear the tenth hurdle, but by then her momentum was lost and the rest of the field surged past her in the final 11.5 metres to the finish.

As Jones crossed the finish line, she sank to the track, her head buried in disbelief for several seconds. She finally lifted her head and watched the video board for verification. Then she buried her head again and broke into a pained crawl, while pounding her right fist into the track. When she lifted her head again, tears were streaking down her face.

Later that day in an interview, Jones said, 'As I

crossed the line it was very hard to pick myself back up – but what can you do but try again?'

The Christian journey will always involve hurdles. They are designed by the enemy to slow us down and ultimately cause us to stumble and fall. The enemy puts them there to keep us from running swiftly, with the hope that eventually we will become so discouraged that we will give up altogether. We can call them hurdles, obstacles, mountains, walls or barriers, but they all have the same purpose and design: to take you out of the race.

God, however, in His wisdom, may permit these hurdles to be placed in our way. His purpose, unlike Satan's, is to use the very same challenge that comes our way as a test of faith, with the hope that it will strengthen our dependence on, and trust in, Him.

So do you look at obstacles in your life as a hindrance? Or do you embrace them for the challenges that they are? Do you shy away from confrontation? Or do you face your fears head-on?

While many choose to avoid the hurdles which stand before them, it is important that we take the right approach.

Put things into perspective

Whether you're dealing with the death of a loved one, a break-up, the loss of a job, a financial dilemma or some other personal problem, all hurdles are meant to be overcome. In order to do so, it is essential that you take the right attitude. How many times are we guilty of allowing our thoughts to sabotage our journey before it even begins?

When you expect to fail, you dramatically decrease your chances of overcoming the obstacles that stand in your way.

Without proper perspective, hurdles are often made to be larger than they really are. However, when we line them up in the light of what God says, we can approach them in their proper context. When it comes to being overwhelmed with problems to the point of giving up, we must remember that the Lord will never bring upon us a situation we cannot overcome with His help. Hear what He promises us:

'The temptations in your life are no different from what others experience. And God is faithful. He will not allow the temptation to be more than you can stand. When you are tempted, he will show you a way out so that you can endure' (1 Corinthians 10:13, NLT).

Are you in a difficult situation and wondering why? The answer from the Lord to you is: 'I trust you, that is why. I would not have given it to you if I didn't know you were equal to it.'

An example of this can be seen through the story of Job.

The example of Job

The first chapter of the book of Job begins by telling us that he lived in the land of Uz, and that he was perfect, that he was upright and that he feared God. Job was blessed with a large family: seven sons and three daughters. He had many possessions, he had a great household and he was 'the greatest of all the men of the east' (vs. 3, KJV).

Since there was no man on Earth like Job, there was a conversation about him between the Lord and Satan. It is interesting to have an opportunity to listen in on a conversation the Lord had with Satan, our adversary and opponent in our Christian journey. Job, of course, was unaware of this conversation.

Satan explained why he believed Job feared God, was upright and perfect, and turned away from evil. He told the Lord it was because He had put a fence around him, his house and all that he had. Satan told God that if He touched all that Job had, Job would curse God to His face.

What he was asking the Lord to do was to remove the protective fence around Job so he could be put to the test. Satan felt that Job had everything, including an easy life with no problems. In other words, who wouldn't serve God when everything is going well? Once Job had experienced tragedy, he wouldn't serve

God anymore and would blame God for it.

So the Lord gave Satan permission to touch everything that Job had, but not to touch him. Satan is always trying to get permission from God to put hurdles in our way.

Tests of life

Our Christian journey can be a similar test of faith. Will we surmount our hurdles? Freeze in front of them? Complain? Or would we continue to serve God if He allowed tragedies to occur in our lives, especially if we were walking uprightly?

So one day, while Job's sons and daughters were spending time together at a feast, a messenger came to Job and told him that the Sabeans had attacked, taking his oxen and slaying his servants. While this person was speaking another messenger came through with news of further calamities, and then another, and then another – this time with news of a disaster resulting in the death of all his sons and daughters. Within a matter of minutes, Job lost everything he had. It was not a gradual loss spanning decades. It happened all at once.

Job did not know it was a test. He did not know about the conversation about him that the Lord had with Satan. Most likely he had never seen or heard of anyone who was righteous, or even unrighteous, losing everything in a matter of minutes.

Yet his response in all of this (Job 1:20-22) indicates that Job did not get angry with the Lord. Instead he fell down on the ground and worshipped Him. He also thanked and blessed the Lord, because he realised that everything he had had been given to him by the Lord. He came into this world with nothing, and he would leave with nothing. Job proved his faithfulness and confirmed God's trust in him. Even when a second wave of tests came his way, leading to him being covered in boils, Job still remained faithful.

Come forth as gold

We don't know how long Job suffered so severely, but it was a very intense hurdle to deal with. But through everything Job proclaimed: 'Though he slay me, yet will I trust in him' (Job 13:15, KJV). The word 'trust' in this verse is the Hebrew word *yachal*, which means 'to wait with hope'.

When we are going through our tests and trials, we will experience various challenges in which we will be able neither to explain nor to understand the reason why. They may last minutes, hours, days, months, years or even a lifetime. It's in times like this that we have to exercise our spiritual armoury, in waiting upon the Lord with the hope that our deliverance will soon come. It's while we are going through our testing trials that God begins to teach us about Himself, and that we see Him in a deeper and clearer way.

When Job's suffering was over, he was given twice as much as before. Job 42:12 (KJV) says, 'So the LORD blessed the latter end of Job more than his beginning'. God gave Job more after his calamities than he had before his calamities. This gives us the assurance that the end reward to be gained, in learning from whatever we have been through, will make us stronger and more resilient, both in life generally and in our spiritual walk with God.

While in Beijing, one of the interviews I had the opportunity of conducting was with Great Britain's 400-metre runner Christine Ohuruogu. I knew she was a Christian, so I was keen to hear how God was making a difference in her life as an athlete. It was encouraging to talk to her about her faith, and how she believed God had given her the gift to run. On the morning of her final 400-metre race I felt impressed to send her a text with the message of one of my favourite Bible passages:

'I can do all things through Christ which strengtheneth me.' (Philippians 4:13, KJV.)

Later that day, Christine went on to win gold in the 400-metre race, beating her closest rival, the USA's Sanya Richards. It was a jubilant day for Great Britain to win its first track and field medal. After the race I got a chance to talk to her about her victory. She told me how that morning she was feeling quite low and despondent about the whole race. She lacked any zeal or energy, and was very discouraged. It was at that time that she read the text message that I had sent at that precise moment: 'I can do all things through Christ which strengtheneth me.' She said, 'It came just at the right time; that was what helped me gain belief in God's ability to use my gift for His glory.'

There was a hurdle in her way that morning, a wave of inadequacy, a momentary loss of confidence. But, through that promise of God, she refocused her thinking – not on her own feelings, but on God's Word. She galvanised her mental strength, and claimed victory over that hurdle, and victory in the race.

We all encounter problems at one time or another. It's a natural part of life. Our sense of success and achievement only comes about through recognising potential obstacles in life and meeting the challenges posed by them head-on. This is what separates those who are successful and have happy lives from others who shy away from difficulties, see themselves as victims and fail to achieve much in life.

Recognise potential stumbling blocks

Occasionally in life, we encounter difficulties at extremely short notice, which doesn't give us any time to prepare for them – and it's during those periods when our strength of character is often put to the greatest test.

Thinking about the things which make us stronger in life enables us to recognise events in which we may be faced with a challenge to overcome. For example, when we face danger, we learn courage; when we endure suffering, we learn patience; when illness hits us, it teaches us how to value our health. Basically, without hurdles and obstacles to overcome, we cannot possibly ever become strong people. How can we know happiness in this fallen world if we haven't experienced sadness? How do we taste the sweetness in life without ever having tasted the bitter?

There are many people who just hope and pray for an easy life. However, what we should be asking for is the strength of character to be able to deal with all of life's adversities instead.

Face your hurdles

Although each of us will experience unique hurdles and obstacles in life, they will often be rooted in similar causes. Take fear, for example; this is a natural human reaction to danger. But fear can also be used as an excuse to avoid the resolution of a particular issue. While this state of inertia may keep us safe for a while, it will also prevent us from taking risks in life which are necessary if we want to overcome a particular problem and experience increased self-confidence.

Sometimes our lack of knowledge, focus and clarity can also confuse us into making a mountain out of a molehill and lead us into a state of virtual paralysis, whereby we end up like a scared rabbit trapped in the headlights, unable to see a way of escape. However, if you think of an obstacle as something you need to get around (or over) in order to progress, it can fuel your determination.

Obstacles can force us to go above and beyond our sense of our own capabilities, and push us to exceed even our wildest expectations.

The result is that we become stronger people, and learn to amass a set of coping tools that will help us when we are faced with even greater challenges in later life.

Cut your hurdles down to their right size

Gaining clarity on an obstacle is crucial in order for us to address it. At the first sense that some kind of problem is about to emerge, some people will completely 'overcook' it and build it up into some kind of insurmountable, Everest-type hurdle that is impossible to get over. However, by writing down your potential hurdles and discussing them with others, you often find that they are not as big as you first perceived.

By breaking the obstacle down into smaller chunks, you make the steps you need to take to overcome them seem a lot smaller and more manageable, too. As you start to formulate some kind of strategy, this process will be retained by you and you will be able to use it and modify it, again and again, when you are faced with other challenges later on.

Learn from your mistakes

You also need to set aside enough time to focus on any particular stumbling block. Don't procrastinate and put off tackling difficulties and think, 'Oh, I'd rather do something more enjoyable today and come back to this later.' In adopting such an approach, you can often make the obstacle or problem bigger and more time-consuming to resolve. So it's always best to tackle it head-on, sooner rather than later!

Think about your fears and worries in general, and address them by following God's method of dealing with them. His promise is: 'Cast your burden upon the LORD and He will sustain you' (Psalm 55:22, NASB).

Sometimes we are faced with the same obstacle more than once, or one which is similar to one we have struggled with in the past. When it occurs, it's important that you are ready for it the second time around and meet it head-on. Never let yourself think that your failure one time will make you bound to fail again.

This time round, the circumstances are likely to be different – and you will also have grown in character through lessons you have learned since the last time. There are many examples of characters in the Bible – for example, Moses, Rahab, Samson, and so on – who experienced huge failures and disappointments, yet went on to be men and women of great faith and spiritual strength.

Finally, overcoming a stumbling block is not always about an outright 'win'. Sometimes you may get over an obstacle, yet feel bumped and bruised along the way. The important thing is that you have still overcome it, and the lessons you have learned in doing so will help you to refine your technique and do it even better next time round.

chapter five

Don't get distracted

Overcoming personal weaknesses that slow you down

At the time of the Olympic Games in Los Angeles in 1984, Zola Budd was the most talked-about athlete in the world. By the standards of her life over the previous few months, nobody could have imagined how the events of 11 August would unfold.

Budd, a petite South African distance runner of outstanding quality, competed barefooted, and stunned the athletic world at the start of that year by breaking the 5,000-metre world record by more than six seconds. She ran it in 15 minutes, 1.83 seconds, to shatter the record held by the American Mary Decker.

South Africa was not allowed to compete at the Olympics because of its apartheid policies, but Budd had a British-born grandfather and, with a great deal of help from a tabloid newspaper which allegedly paid £100,000 for her story, she was brought to England under a veil of secrecy, and fast-tracked into becoming a British citizen. She quickly proved her athletic ability and was selected to compete for Great Britain at the Olympics.

The final of the 3,000-metre race was held in the Memorial Coliseum. The home fans were expecting a gold medal from Decker. She liked to run from the front, as did Budd, and by the time the field entered the home straight, with just over three laps to go, the pair had already shared an exchange after bumping into each other. Budd led Decker, with Romania's Maricica Puica behind. There was a tangle; Decker's leg touched Budd's foot; the pair lost balance; Decker caught Budd's trailing leg – and the American fell, careering off the track and into the infield.

Boos rang out around the stadium. Decker was out of the race, and Budd dropped back to finish seventh as Puica won in 8 minutes, 35.96 seconds. After the race, Budd went to apologise, but Decker told her she was not interested.

Decker vowed in front of the cameras that she would never, ever forgive Zola Budd for what she did. Years later, the feud still continued.

A simple statement of regret for her harsh words – and for laying the full blame upon Britain's Zola Budd after their famous collision – could have saved Decker from a cascade of criticism: reprimands from fellow runners, and spoof awards for being Whiner of the

Year (*USA Today*) and The Year's Sorest Loser
(*Esquire*). But Decker remained adamant. 'I don't feel
that I have any reason to apologise; I was the one who
was wronged.'

Decker continued her running career, but things
were never the same.

She had suffered a series of stress-induced
fractures on her legs, and she agreed to have a
sequence of more than thirty orthopaedic procedures.
She made further attempts to run competitively in
marathons; however, the surgery just increased the
occurrence of the problems. She was forced to retire
from athletics, and she can now only jog occasionally.

Mary Decker's athletic career was short-lived. It
seemed that, from that fateful collision with Zola Budd,
every time she ran she carried the burden of
resentment and unforgiveness. Who knows whether
this indirectly contributed to her stress-induced
fractures?

Lay aside the weight

We are admonished in Scripture to '. . . lay aside
every weight, and the sin which so easily ensnares us,
and let us run with endurance the race that is set
before us' (Hebrews 12:1, NKJV).

In order to run effectively and swiftly in the Christian
race, we have to let go of the things in life that are

slowing us down.

Athletes today recognise that by wearing designer ultra-lightweight trainers, they might be able to shave a hundredth of a second off their personal best.

The apostle Paul, during his missionary travels, took note of athletes as they prepared for the ancient games – and he made important comparisons between running and the Christian life.

Paul begins by saying we must 'lay aside every weight'. Why is that? Because weights slow you down. The word rendered 'weight' – (Greek: ὄγκον ogkon) – means what is crooked or hooked, and therefore anything that is attached or suspended by a hook.

Snares of the devil

In the last chapter we learnt that Satan's desire is to impede us by placing hurdles in our way – hurdles designed to make us fall and stay down. His other strategy is to get us hooked into negative patterns of behaviour. For each person there are different hooks. For one person it may be unforgiveness, like Decker; in another, lust; in another, a violent and almost ungovernable temper; for others, it could be worry, anxiety or fear.

Whatever it may be, we are exhorted to 'lay it aside' – and this general direction may be applied to anything which prevents us from running freely.

Besetting sins

Paul continues in Hebrews 12:1 (KJV) by saying, 'and the sin which doth so easily beset us.'

The word rendered 'easily beset' denotes the sin which especially wraps itself around us, to hinder our course, and alludes to the way long oriental garments were worn.

The runner would be careful not to encumber himself with a garment which could wind around his legs while he was running, and hinder him. So it is with the Christian, who should lay aside everything which may hinder him – that is, any sin which impedes his course. Such sins are appropriately called 'easily besetting sins'. They are those that we find more difficult to overcome, and to which we are particularly and personally vulnerable.

They are such sins as the following:

=**1**= Those to which you are particularly exposed by your natural temperament, such as anger, selfishness, pride and egocentricity.

=**2**= Those in which you freely indulged before you became a Christian – and which can return through careless association with others. The temptation to return to these sins will arise from time to time, and they need to be confessed and forsaken.

=**3**= Sins to which we are particularly susceptible as a result of areas of weakness in our lives. All of us, if we are honest, have some weakness – and it is here that we can be particularly vulnerable. It is important to be fully aware of such weaknesses, and constantly look to God to be guarded and strengthened in those areas.

Breaking the bondage

Mary Decker struggled with unforgiveness. It wasn't until many years later that she and Zola Budd shook hands again. But unforgiveness is one besetment that can really slow us down. While I was pastoring in the west of England, there was one regular visitor to my congregation who had lost her son from a drug overdose.

It seemed that the pain and turmoil of this sad loss was re-lived every week, and Mary appeared sullen and withdrawn each time she came to church. I arranged a meeting with her, and she shared with me how she was finding it difficult to cope. She missed her son terribly, but felt hatred and envy towards his two surviving friends, who were with him at the time. She believed that they had led him to his death.

These feelings of hurt and pain were like a thicket of brambles entangling her, choking out her joy and happiness. Her Christian journey was a painful one. There was no freedom in her life. The emotional and mental struggle of grappling with resentment, anger, malice and the desire for vengeance wore her down to the point of depression. She was truly weighed down by this besetment.

I arranged a follow-up meeting with her, during which we addressed the whole area of forgiveness. Towards the end of this meeting, I asked her to write down all the names of those whom the Holy Spirit brought to mind who needed her forgiveness. After a moment of silence, during which she listened to the voice of God, she wrote twenty-five names on her list: the last three of which were those of the two boys who were with her son on the day he died – and lastly her son's own name.

We went through each name on the list, and Mary said a simple but meaningful prayer:

'Lord, I choose to forgive_____ (mention the name) for _____ (say how they hurt you and how it made you feel).'

She prayed this prayer for every name on her list. It was an emotionally painful experience, but as we went further down the list I could sense her relief and her release from the burden. As each name was verbalised, her face showed the pain it caused and the bitterness of the mental picture that was formed in her mind as she recalled the event. Then came the picture of calm as she renounced any hatred for that person.

The Christian Race

As we came down to the last three names, Mary began to struggle to mention the name of the first of the two boys. I prayed silently and earnestly, realising that the enemy did not want her to be released from this bondage.

Tears streamed down her cheeks as she momentarily re-lived all the pain that had been caused by the boys. But, as she persevered, the Spirit of God prevailed, and she went through the prayer with each of them. It seemed, at last, that all her anguish would disappear now that those names were released. Unknown to us, however, the real struggle came when Mary tried to mention her own son. There was an unseen spiritual battle taking place in her heart. All the time, the real cause of her bitterness and anger had been not so much the two other boys, but her own son. Deep within her heart, she harboured a strong unforgiving spirit towards the one who had been the object of her love.

'Lord, I choose to forgive my son', she said, in a weakened voice. By now Mary's hands were shaking, her lips quivering, as it dawned on her what had really been causing her depression.

Her prayer continued: '. . . for being rebellious toward me; for blaming me for leaving his father and taking it out on drugs; for making me feel so inadequate, and ashamed that I could not be a better mother, and that I was not there to help him.'

When Mary finished this last prayer, I couldn't help noticing that she gave a deep sigh of release. Her burden was lifted. She was free in Christ. Her sullen and frowning expression gave way to one of peace. A smile came over her face; she knew it was all over. The weight that had weighed her down was lifted. The enemy no longer had her bound. It was as quick as that. Her freedom came when she was willing to move towards forgiveness and express it in a sincere way.

Forgiveness is a process. There may be experiences you have been through that are deep-rooted, and the cause of much intense hurt and pain: memories that you would rather suppress, never to let them return to your consciousness. I believe that God understands how difficult it is to forgive instantaneously. He is a gracious God, and He works with our limitations. If we allow Him to break down our barriers and soothe our emotional scars with His promises of being near to the broken-hearted and close to those who are bruised in spirit, the Spirit of God can lead us to the point where we harbour no ill feelings toward anyone, and give us the power to forgive, just as we have been forgiven by our heavenly Father. Our freedom begins when we choose to start this process.

The Christian Race

Sins of the flesh

Other besetments that can slow us down are those things 'pleasing to the senses', that are designed to hinder our spiritual journey. These can lead to addictions such as drugs, alcohol, smoking, gambling or pornography – all of which can become 'weights' that we might be hooked on.

Let's remember that the term 'besetting sin' refers to a habitual sin: one that can have a strong hold on us, causing us to fall back into it time and time again. This can be a particular sin that has an especially strong hold upon us, and one that the enemy may use to convince us that we are unworthy to serve the Lord.

What is a besetting sin to one person may not trouble another at all. Practically every believer wrestles with persistent sin of some kind, even those whose service to Christ is of outstanding quality. The besetting sin is both perplexing and harassing, and, if allowed to linger and grow, may end in tragic moral failure.

Examples of besetting sin: Moses' explosive temper and David's weakness for women. When they grew weak in their faith and weary in their warfare against evil, their besetting sins rose up to challenge them.

Also, the besetting sin may occur after a long time of spiritual victory. It may not become obvious until we really desire to serve God and seriously seek His face.

When it confronts us, it causes us to doubt our worthiness in serving God. David's sin of adultery immediately followed one of his greatest victories. However, his fall was preceded by other 'weights' which were ensnaring and which led to his besetting sin.

These smaller sins, or 'weights', then stimulate the besetting sin to reappear – and the believer finds himself in a struggle for his soul again.

Our besetting sin can either drive us closer to God, if we go to Him for help when we need it, or drive us away from God, if we continually submit to its desires.

Overcoming besetments

Is there hope of being free from besetting sin? Of course. Paul says in Romans 7:19-25 (NIV): 'For what I do is not the good I want to do; no, the evil I do not want to do – this I keep on doing. Now if I do what I do not want to do, it is no longer I who do it, but it is sin living in me that does it. So I find this law at work: When I want to do good, evil is right there with me. For in my inner being I delight in God's law; but I see another law at work in the members of my body, waging war against the law of my mind and making me a prisoner of the law of sin at work within my members. What a wretched man I am! Who will rescue me from this body of death? Thanks be to God –

through Jesus Christ our Lord!'

You can't simply just walk away from besetting sin – you must learn to hate your sin the way God hates your sin. Many secretly cherish and love their sin, and so fall prey to it later at a weak moment. You must desire to live a holy life before God, and to give up your sin. Ask God if you have a besetting sin that is keeping you from being totally free. Ask Him to help you see the sin the way He sees it. Be convinced that God loves you in spite of your sin. Although He absolutely hates all sin, He is infinite in His love and compassion for you. We must accept the help of God in resisting and overcoming.

David Wilkerson (in 'Victory Over Your Besetting Sin' – *http://www.worldchallenge.org/en/node/1342*) likens a besetting sin to an octopus with many tentacles, trying to crush out our lives: 'Seldom do all tentacles loosen their hold at once. It is one tentacle at a time.' We must realise that it is not in our own strength that sin is to be conquered, but through Christ's victory over sin on the cross. It is for us, however, to choose to let the light into the secret places of our hearts where sin may lurk, waiting for an opportune moment to appear. This may be, as said earlier, at a weak moment or after a great victory. Deal with sin ruthlessly, completely. See it for what it is. I once heard a speaker liken our love of sin to seeing a giant poisonous spider and embracing it and kissing it, even though, in the end, it would destroy us.

God, however, has the final say, and the final victory over sin is ours if we want it. As a bonus, when we achieve victory over besetting and habitual sin, other enemies in our lives may flee as well: worry, fear, guilt, anxiety, depression, restlessness and loneliness.

God desires holiness, not just for His sake, but to set us free from the forces which seek to destroy us.

Let it go

When I was in the Marshall Islands as a student missionary, one of the things I enjoyed when we had free time was snorkelling. The tropical climate, together with the coral formation of the island, made a perfect recipe for spotting the most beautiful coloured fish in the sea. We were warned by the principal of the church school where we were teaching not to go out snorkelling or swimming on our own, because of the deceptive low tides and strong currents.

It was a warning I failed to heed, believing there was not too much to be worried about. So one Sunday afternoon I went off by myself to the end of the island, where at low tide you could walk quite a good distance with the water only as high as your knees. I snorkelled around the area for a while, swimming out about 50 metres, when I spotted two beautifully coloured shells submerged on the sea bed. I dived down, and, for sure, these large shells were absolutely stunning! The colours, red, blue and green, were all reminiscent of the rainbow.

It was a sight to behold. I marked the spot where they were and continued swimming around for a while, before returning to the exact spot to take them back to the campus. My only thought was, *Wait till everyone sees what I've found!* I swooped down, and with one shell in each hand made an attempt to swim back to the shore. By this time the tide had begun drawing in, and, whereas before the sea had reached my knees, now it was up to my neck. Still confident in my swimming skills, I proceeded to swim with shells in hand. They were quite heavy and prevented me from cutting through the water effectively with my front crawl. I considered dropping the shells and using both hands to swim back to shore. But no, I wanted to take those shells back to show everyone what I'd found. I swam with all my strength, but it seemed that I was not gaining ground. The side current was now pushing me further along the beach, and the impulse to drop the shells and swim to safety returned, but was cancelled again.

I remember thinking there could be sharks out there, but even that thought did not make me release the shells. After twenty minutes of hard, laborious swimming, I finally made it back to shore, albeit a long way from where I started. I dropped to the sandy shore tired and exhausted, with my heart beating very fast. But I had done it!

After having gained my breath and recovered somewhat, I turned over to look at the shells for which I had almost drowned. To my utter surprise the 'beautiful' shells that I had seen in the water were now grey, slimy and darkened. I couldn't believe it! In the water they looked so beautiful. Maybe because the water refracted sunlight like a prism, the shells looked awesome, but now they were out of the water they were no more than two ordinary, mundane objects with no attraction whatsoever.

What I thought was pleasing and attractive turned out to be nothing more than a distraction. Yet I could have lost my life for them!

The apostle Paul knew exactly what he was talking about when he advised us to let go of the things that are slowing us down. It's time to take a good look in the mirror. Let's be honest with ourselves. What things are you holding onto that need to be relinquished? What are the besetting sins that you seem almost powerless to resist? Let the Holy Spirit reveal to you which areas in your life contain 'extra baggage'. Now let the same Holy Spirit give you the conviction and the power to help you remove them from your life.

Cast all the excess weight on Him. God can handle it. Let Him take away all your burdens.

I guarantee that, once you do this, you will breathe a deep sigh of relief. The bonds that the enemy would have you tied up with will finally be released, and you will be able to experience newness of life and true freedom as you continue along in the Christian journey.

How to be victorious

Here are some steps you can take to help you deal with the 'weight' and 'besetting sins' that impede your walk with God:

=*1*= First, you must admit that you are stuck in your besetting sin and cannot help yourself. Quit trying to overcome it in your own strength. Give up! Give your burden to the Lord. Come to Jesus like you are and call out to Him from deep within your heart, 'Jesus, heal me and I will be healed. Save me and I will be saved. You alone are my Salvation and my Hope.'

=*2*= Own up – acknowledge and confess your sins. If you are solely, utterly, simply and totally focused on God, then He will come to you. James 4:8 (KJV): 'Draw nigh to God, and he will draw nigh to you.'

Pray this: 'Lord Jesus, I confess pride, self-sufficiency and independence from You in the lifestyle I have lived. I lay my life totally in Your hands and claim

Your promise that You will deliver me from all evil.'

=*3*= Commit yourself to a disciplined lifestyle. How desperate are you to be free? When you are sick and tired of being sick and tired, then you will do everything necessary to commit to Jesus.

Pray this prayer aloud: 'Lord, convict me and bring me to the place where I am willing to do anything You ask, even to the point of denying my flesh and taking up my cross daily.'

=*4*= Ask Jesus to give you His rest. He says to each of us, 'Come unto me, all ye that labour and are heavy laden, and I will give you rest.' (Matthew 11:28, KJV.)

I pray that, as you pray these things, God will give you His hope and courage within your spirit – and that, from this moment on, you will never again believe the lie of Satan that you can't overcome your addictions. You have listened to the devil too long; now take the Word of God to heart – believe it, and act upon it.

Second Corinthians 2:14 (KJV): 'Now thanks be unto God, which always causeth us to triumph in Christ, and maketh manifest the savour of his knowledge by us in every place.'

chapter six

Run to finish

Perseverance – enduring until the end

G reat Britain's Derek Redmond may not be someone whose name conjures up memories of Olympic medals or world records, but he is someone who defines the essence of the Olympic spirit.

Redmond arrived at the 1992 Olympic Games in Barcelona determined to win a medal in the 400 metres. He had been forced to withdraw from the 400 metres at the 1988 Games in Seoul, only ten minutes before the race, because of an Achilles tendon injury. He underwent five operations over the next year, and when the 1992 Games arrived they were expected to provide his final chance to make an impact and to fulfil his dream of winning a medal.

Derek's father, Jim, had accompanied him to Barcelona, just as he did for all world competitions. They were as close as a father and son could be, inseparable, and the best of friends. When Derek ran, it was as if his father was running right next to him.

The day of the race arrived. Father and son reminisced about what it had taken for Derek to get to this point. They talked about ignoring past heartbreaks and past failures. They agreed that if anything bad happened, no matter what it was, Derek had to finish the race!

The top four finishers in each of the two semi-final heats would qualify for the Olympic final. As race time approached for the 400-metre semi-final heat, Jim headed up to his seat at the top of the Olympic Stadium, not far from where the Olympic torch had been lit just a few days earlier. The stadium was packed with 65,000 spectators, bracing themselves for one of sport's greatest and most exciting events.

Soon after the race began, Redmond broke from the pack and quickly seized the lead. Down the back straight, only 175 metres away from finishing, Redmond looked certain to make the finals. Suddenly, he heard a 'pop' in his right hamstring. He pulled up lame, as if he had been shot. His leg quivering, Redmond began hopping on one leg, then slowed down and fell to the ground.

As he lay on the track clutching his right hamstring, one of the medical personnel ran towards him. At the same time, Jim Redmond, seeing his son in trouble, raced down from the top row of the stands, sidestepping people and bumping into others. He had no credential to be on the track, but all he could think about was getting to his son, to help him up. 'I wasn't going to be stopped by anyone', he later told the media.

Down on the track, Redmond realised his dream of an Olympic medal was shattered. Tears streamed down his face. All he could think was, *I'm out of the Olympics – again!*

As the medical crew arrived with a stretcher, Redmond told them, 'No, there's no way I'm getting on that stretcher. I'm going to finish my race.'

Then, in a moment that will live forever in the minds of millions, Redmond lifts himself to his feet, ever so slowly, and starts hobbling down the track. The other runners have finished the race, with Steve Lewis of the US winning the contest in 44.50 seconds. Suddenly, everyone realises that Redmond isn't dropping out of the race by hobbling off to the side of the track. No, he is actually continuing on one leg! He's going to attempt to hobble his way to the finish line. All by himself. All in the name of perseverance.

Slowly, the crowd, in total disbelief, rises and begins to cheer. The cheer gets louder and louder. Through the searing pain, Redmond hears the roars, but 'I wasn't doing it for the crowd,' he would later say, 'I was doing it for me. Whether people thought I was an idiot or a hero, I wanted to finish the race.'

One painful step at a time, each one a little slower and more painful than the one before, Redmond limps onward and the crowd urges him on.

Jim Redmond finally gets to the bottom of the stands, leaps over the railing, avoids a security guard, and runs out to his son, with two security guards chasing after him. 'That's my son out there,' he yells back to security, 'and I'm going to help him!'

Finally, with Derek refusing to surrender and painfully limping along the track, Jim reaches his son at the final bend, about 120 metres from the finish, and wraps his arm around his waist.

'I'm here, son', Jim says softly, hugging his boy. 'We'll finish together.' Derek puts his arms around his father's shoulders and sobs.

Together, arm-in-arm, with 65,000 people cheering and clapping, father and son finish the race just as they vowed they would. A couple of steps from the finish line, Jim releases the grip he has on his son, so Derek can cross the finish line by himself. Then he throws his arms around Derek again, both crying, along with everyone in the stands and on TV.

'I'm the proudest father alive', he tells the press afterwards, tears in his eyes. 'I'm prouder of him than I would have been if he had won the gold medal. It took a lot of guts for him to do what he did.'

Derek Redmond ran the slowest 400 metres in

The Christian Race

Olympic history – it took him about five minutes to finish! Because he had been helped, the space next to his name was marked 'AB' – Abandoned.

But Derek Redmond had not abandoned his race. Indeed, not! Neither had he abandoned his purpose, his goal or his reason for going to those Olympic Games. Most certainly, his father did not abandon him.

'If anything happened, he had to finish', Jim Redmond said. 'We had an agreement.'

'We started your career together', his father told him when he joined him on the track. 'We will finish this race together.'

What an awesome display of courage and persistence. For me this is probably one of the greatest sporting moments. There are so many spiritual parallels here. We see commitment, determination, and most of all perseverance.

The apostle Paul in his writings continues the Olympic theme by admonishing us to 'lay aside every weight, and the sin which so easily ensnares us,' and to 'run with endurance the race that is set before us, looking unto Jesus' (Hebrews 12:1, 2, NKJV). The NIV translation says, '. . . and let us run with perseverance'. Jesus, talking of perseverance, says: '. . . he who endures to the end will be saved.' (Matthew 10:22, NKJV.)

If we are to strive to the end we need to 'stay in the game', no matter how hard it gets. On the Christian journey we will encounter many surprises: joys and times of despair; ups and downs. It is a reflection of life; anything can happen. The question we need to ask ourselves is this: 'Am I willing to keep running when things are not going the way I want them to?'

Perseverance is the single-minded desire of the heart that, come what may, by the strength of God implanted within me, I will hold onto Jesus and put my explicit trust in Him. It says that my desire to keep going is not influenced by what happens around me, but by the Lord, who is living within me. My direction is not dictated or controlled by the circumstances in life, but I allow the Lord to control the direction of my life. I live and move forward because I have a good reason to be doing so. The reason for this is not based on any temporal experiences that may be here today and gone tomorrow. My decision is based on eternal principles; it goes beyond this life, to the life to come. It is a hope that keeps me focused and allows me to endure the momentary difficulties that come upon us. You'll find that you have a bigger goal and a larger vision! Perseverance is what happens when we allow nothing to stop us from obtaining this higher glory. For Derek Redmond it was a relentless desire to cross the finish line in an athletic competition. For us it is a relentless desire to cross a different finishing line.

Paul expressed this accomplishment as he was

nearing the end of his life when he said, 'I have fought the good fight, I have finished the race'. In other words, 'I have held on to what I believe to be true and have "kept the faith".' The reward for such faithfulness is a 'crown of righteousness'. (2 Timothy 4:7, 8, NKJV.)

Perseverance is the key if we are going to endure to the end. Getting back up when we fall down is not easy. Our heavenly Father knows that we will have our knocks and setbacks. That's why Proverbs tells us that, though a 'righteous man may fall seven times', because he knows he has a forgiving and patient Father, he will 'rise again' (Proverbs 24:16, NKJV). Failure is not in the 'falling down', but in the 'not getting back up'.

The Christian walk is about continuing. We sin every day, be it in thought or action, but we have to come to Christ in a spirit of repentance and seek His forgiveness and mercy. His promise is that, 'If we confess our sins, He is faithful and just to forgive us our sins and to cleanse us from all unrighteousness' (1 John 1:9, NKJV). A key word here is 'cleanse'. Christ not only wants to forgive us, but also to restore us to a point of taking away the desire to go back to what made us fall in the first place.

Despite every challenge, Christ encourages us to keep going. However, the reality is that there are times when discouragement comes, and this can lead us to give up in the spiritual journey.

Despondency is the feeling of despair in the face of obstacles. It is an overwhelming sensation that grows out of disappointment, unmet expectations or failed relationships. It often accompanies depression or failure.

There are a number of biblical characters who experienced this – one of whom was Elijah.

Elijah, the great man of God, had just experienced some of the most dramatic challenges and victories of his life (1 Kings 18).

He served a God who, in answer to his prayer, sent fire down from Heaven to light his altar. He personally took all of the false prophets of Baal and destroyed them. A great victory had been won for the cause of righteousness. Immediately after defeating the prophets of Baal and humiliating his worshippers, Elijah called an end to the drought by praying for rain – a prayer which the Lord answered.

Yet despite these miraculous displays of God's power, there was no reformation or revival among the people. It appeared that no one understood what God had done and was planning to do.

In addition to this, when his life was threatened by Jezebel, King Ahab's wife, Elijah fled for his life.

We now see him sitting down under a broom tree and praying that he might die: 'It is enough! Now, LORD, take my life, for I am no better than my fathers!' (1 Kings 19:4, NKJV.)

The Christian Race

All of a sudden Elijah felt isolated and alone. Immediately after being on the pinnacle of spiritual victory, he seems to plunge into the valley of discouragement.

What could have caused such a dramatic change?

There are several things that we can learn from Elijah's experience.

First, he was physically exhausted. He had ministered before the Lord and the nation. He had spent days in intercessory prayer for Israel and for rain. He stood before the masses of people and rebuked falsehood. He ran ahead of Ahab's chariot to announce that God was sending rain.

Then, he became afraid of the repercussions of his actions and ran a day's journey into the wilderness to escape.

Maybe you have been through times of great physical exhaustion. You may have had several days or weeks of illness, and were not feeling yourself. Your physical reserves were gone. Maybe you had spent several sleepless nights tending to a sick loved one, or just finished going through a trying period of physically challenging work. The days were long and the nights were short. Your body was exhausted. Perhaps you had just finished one huge project when another one was dumped in your lap.

These are signals that indicate the possible onset of

physical burnout and a susceptibility to despondency. We constantly need to take a critical look at what is going on in our lives and guard against such over-exhaustion.

Second, Elijah was emotionally drained. He had just been through a very challenging period of time. Everything that had happened made a negative impact on his emotional wellbeing. He had experienced a tremendous challenge when God told him to present himself to Ahab, who had been killing the Lord's prophets. He experienced an emotional rush when God answered his prayer and fire fell down from Heaven. Now he was emotionally exhausted.

Emotional exhaustion can hit suddenly after a catastrophic event. Many times it is not work that wears us out, but worry, anxiety and fear. These feelings tend to sap our strength and deplete our reserves. Christ constantly encourages us to cast our cares upon Him (1 Peter 5:7), and to take His yoke upon us in exchange for our burdens (Matthew 11:28-30). We are also asked not to worry about tomorrow (Matthew 6:25-34) because He will provide for us.

Third, Elijah lost his spiritual focus. He had demonstrated extreme faith, fortitude and zeal. He stood up for God without the encouragement of others. Jezebel had been hunting down the prophets of God to kill them. Now, Elijah lost his spiritual perspective.

Apparently, he had forgotten the power of Almighty God. He simply told God he was ready to give up and end it all. He had lost his spiritual vigour. Doubt had replaced faith and Elijah had come down from the mountain, from being a conqueror to being conquered.

Satan is always on the lookout for our times of physical, emotional and spiritual vulnerability so that he can launch an attack. We have to be on our guard against him. The spiritual weapons of warfare are there for us to use to avoid the 'fiery darts' of the enemy. (Ephesians 6:10-17, KJV.)

Elijah also had unmet expectations. He thought there would be a mass revival following his mountaintop ministry and that the nation would return to the true God and reject idolatry. Who would blame him after witnessing what God had done? However, it did not happen quite as fast as Elijah had wanted.

Maybe you have prayed but your prayers have not yet been answered. Or you may have sought divine guidance, and the direction given was not what you expected. Maybe you still find yourself struggling with sin, and each time you 'fall' it leaves you thinking, 'I just can't go on anymore.'

Maybe the trial you are going through is so overwhelming that it seems you can't bear it and you're no longer hearing from God. The world presses in on you and you begin to think of how much easier it would be just to give up and to do your own thing, live your own life!

Well, maybe that option seems easier, but perseverance recognises that there will be many falls and setbacks, many periods of frustration and feelings of guilt. There will be times of just wanting to abandon the faith, or of feeling trapped in the belief that you are simply not good or worthy enough to be called a Christian.

Either way, disillusionment can set in, leading to discouragement if we are not willing to trust God's timing and His way of leading us.

God really does understand the way we feel. He knows the depths of our grief and pain. He is patient towards us in our times of disobedience and rebelliousness. He continues to be merciful in times of guilt and shame, and is gracious in allowing us to have another chance.

We tend to forget that God is above and beyond us, and that He knows the best plan of action for our lives. If we remind ourselves that, in every circumstance in life, God already has our best interests at heart, it will help us dismiss negative feelings toward Him.

There are a number of passages of Scripture in which God promises to be with us in our times of need.

Psalm 27:1 (NKJV): 'The LORD is my light and my salvation; Whom shall I fear? The LORD is the strength of my life; Of whom shall I be afraid?'

Psalm 138:7 (NKJV): 'Though I walk in the midst of trouble, You will revive me; You will stretch out Your hand Against the wrath of my enemies, And Your right hand will save me.'

2 Corinthians 4:8, 9 (NIV): 'We are hard pressed on every side, but not crushed; perplexed, but not in despair; persecuted, but not abandoned; struck down, but not destroyed.'

John 14:1 (NIV): 'Do not let your hearts be troubled. Trust in God; trust also in me.'

Philippians 1:6 (NIV): 'being confident of this, that he who began a good work in you will carry it on to completion until the day of Christ Jesus.'

He has not forsaken you. He has not abandoned you. He has been your help and strength and will continue to be so. God's cure for Elijah's despondency involved a renewed purpose and plan for his life. God was not finished with Elijah. Likewise, He has a purpose and a plan for each of us.

Like Derek Redmond's father, God is not a mere spectator in our Christian journey. He is an active Participant with us. He does not stand by on the sidelines watching how we progress – He is Immanuel, 'God with us'.

He says, with His arm placed around us, 'We began this race together: we will finish it together.'

chapter seven

The ultimate prize

Receiving your reward at the end of the race

I had just won my first ever trophy. It was at our inter-college sports day held at the Crystal Palace athletic stadium in London – a venue that has played host to many great athletes and where a number of world records have been set. I had won the men's long jump by just one centimetre. For the first time I stood by the podium, waiting for my name to be called to receive the winner's trophy. Needless to say, I was elated!

'And in first place, the winner, Richard Daly!' There were cheers and applause from the audience and team supporters who travelled with us. There I was, standing on the first-place spot, raising my trophy for the entire crowd to see. It was a jubilant moment for me.

Throughout the return journey to our college in the minibus, I had not let the trophy out of my hands. I kept examining it, turning it around in my hands, making sure there were no marks or scratches on it. It was my prized possession.

Then, all of a sudden, there was a loud screeching sound as the minibus came to an abrupt halt to avoid a collision. As it jerked forward, the next thing I knew the trophy was flying out of my hands. As though in slow motion, it spun around in the air, twisting and turning. I reached out to grab it with both hands, but to no avail; the trophy dropped to the ground and broke in three pieces. That was the end of my trophy; that was the end of my prize. It lasted for the grand duration of just one and a half hours!

The tradition of winners receiving trophies or crowns stems back to the ancient Olympic Games in Greece. According to the Olympic Museum and IOC Studies Centre in Lausanne, the games were held at four different sites – Olympia, Delphi, Corinth and Nemea. Each city would have one winner who would receive the leaf crown for that city. At Olympia, the crown was made of wild olive leaves; at Delphi, laurel leaves; at Corinth, pine leaves; and at Nemea, wild cherry leaves.

Throughout the New Testament the apostle Paul, in reference to his race theme, refers to crowns that will be given to those who are faithful in their spiritual journey until the end.

In 1 Corinthians 9:25 he tells us that this crown is an incorruptible crown. It is a crown that is received by those who have endured the challenges and trials, overcome the hurdles and broken through the pain barrier of hitting 'the wall'. It is worn by those who were prepared to let go of the things that were slowing them down, and allowed the Spirit of God to give them victory over the besetting sins within the Christian race. Therefore, Paul talks about this crown as a 'crown of rejoicing' (1 Thessalonians 2:19, KJV). It is also called a 'crown of righteousness' (2 Timothy 4:8, KJV), because the recipient is clothed with the righteousness of Jesus Christ.

This crown which the Lord gives at the end of the journey is received when He returns in splendour, accompanied by all the angels. This is also referred to fittingly as the 'crown of glory' (1 Peter 5:4, KJV). The most beautiful part of receiving this crown is that it is not given for a momentary experience, but it is called a 'crown of life' (James 1:12, KJV) because it will be ours to keep throughout eternity. Everyone in Heaven will receive one. In the sporting world it is only the winner who receives the trophy. In Christ, however, everyone is a winner and will receive a reward.

You may never have the opportunity of standing on a podium when your name is called in some sports arena to receive a trophy, but infinitely greater is the occasion that will come to you when Jesus Christ Himself will call your name, surrounded by 'so great a cloud of witnesses' (Hebrews 12:1, KJV) to cheer and applaud you. Angels who have witnessed your journey on Earth, your fellow saints – all will attend this great heavenly awards ceremony.

There will be fanfare and trumpet-blowing!

John the Revelator provides us with a glimpse of this day when he says, 'After these things I looked, and behold, a great multitude which no one could number, of all nations, tribes, peoples, and tongues, standing before the throne and before the Lamb, clothed with white robes . . . saying, 'Salvation belongs to our God who sits on the throne, and to the Lamb!' (Revelation 7:9, 10, NKJV.)

When the question was asked as to who these people dressed in white robes are, and where they come from, this answer is given:

'These are the ones who come out of the great tribulation, and washed their robes and made them white in the blood of the Lamb.' (Revelation 7:14, NKJV.)

It depicts what would be a grand closing ceremony to mark the end of life as we know it here on this earth. It also signals an opening ceremony to mark a new life in eternity where we will live and reign with Jesus Christ.

When we take a glimpse of what Heaven will be like, it ought to help us to hold on all the more during the momentary challenges that we face here on Earth. We know that something better will come one day. This is the hope that makes us want to live in life eternal: it is the hope of the promise of the soon return of our Lord and Saviour Jesus Christ.

Why do athletes endure all the tears, sweat and pain of practice after practice? Why do they run endless sprints, lift weight after weight, and go on a special diet? Because they are looking beyond the trials they are undergoing. They look beyond the hardships and strict training regime. They do it to win first place and receive a gold medal.

Likewise, let us look at the other side of the trials and the sufferings we face in this life and on Earth. We are encouraged with those words of hope that say, 'Blessed is the man who perseveres under trial, because when he has stood the test, he will receive the crown of life that God has promised to those who love him' (James 1:12, NIV).

The promise here is not just of a blessing at the end of the journey; there are blessings throughout the journey. God will reward us for being faithful to Him as a way of encouraging us to keep running the race.

The prize Paul speaks of includes a number of rewards given to those who overcome. As well as a crown, winners will also be clothed in white raiment, a symbol of being made pure, and their names will remain written in the book of life (Revelation 3:5) – an honour roll of all who have triumphed.

The overcomer will also have the reward of eating from the tree of life (Revelation 2:7). To those who have made God their first love, this tree will yield twelve types of fruit every month, and the leaves will be for the healing of the nations (Revelation 22:2). God has preserved this tree for His faithful.

The overcomer will also be immortalised in the heavenly wall of fame and be given a new name (Revelation 2:17). The winners of the Olympic Games in ancient Greece became heroes in their home towns. Sometimes the citizens made coins with the image of winners on them in order to remember them and to make them known throughout the Greek world. They also had the privilege of having statues made of them and hearing poets write about their skills.

We are told that overcomers in Christ will also be immortalised. Revelation 3:12 tells us that we will become a permanent part of God's Temple entourage, like a monument that will always be remembered.

Lastly, we are told, 'He who overcomes shall inherit all things, and I will be his God and he shall be My son.' (Revelation 21:7, NKJV.)

The reward is to receive ownership of all that God

has prepared in His Kingdom. This includes the promise of an end to all that we are acquainted with here on Earth as a result of sin. Revelation 21:4 (KJV) tells us, 'And God shall wipe away all tears from their eyes; and there shall be no more death, neither sorrow, nor crying, neither shall there be any more pain: for the former things are passed away.'

In light of this I ask: 'If Olympians can dedicate so much of their lives to such a short-lived victory – if one little medal is that important to them – how much more energy should we devote to a bigger and far more significant race?'

Have you stopped to think about your life as a journey? Are you conscious that you are on a journey now?

Every person, Christian and non-Christian alike, possesses a desire to discover and fulfil his or her purpose in life. Some people align their lives with God's purpose, while others do not. Whether you will find out His plans for your life, and fulfil them, depends on you. It is your responsibility to discover your destiny and make it your calling. God will not violate your will or make you do what you don't want to do. However, without a firm commitment to fulfilling your destiny in Christ, you would go through your journey hoping and wishing that life would be better. There would be emptiness in your soul and lack of fulfilment.

Therefore, I encourage you to make it your decision to find and live out God's plan for your life. Make a resolution to serve the living God with all your heart, with all your strength, and with all your mind.

Christ wants us to inherit His Kingdom, to enjoy all the provisions He has in store for us. We have nothing to lose, but everything to gain.

The final reward is of infinite value – and it's worth the journey!